THE BOOK O
BRITISH MOT(
GEARBOXES AND

CU00820394

ALBION
B.S.A.
BURMAN
DOUGLAS
NEW HUDSON
RUDGE
SCOTT
STURMEY ARCHER
VELOCETTE

A Floyd Clymer 'Motorcyclist's Library' publication
Published in 2018 by: www.VelocePress.com

INTRODUCTION

Welcome to the world of digital publishing ~ the book you now hold in your hand, was printed using the latest state of the art digital technology. The advent of print-on-demand has forever changed the publishing process, never has information been so accessible and it is our hope that this book serves your informational needs for years to come. If this is your first exposure to digital publishing, we hope that you are pleased with the results. Many more titles of interest to the classic automobile and motorcycle enthusiast, collector and restorer are available via our website at www.VelocePress.com. We hope that you find this title as interesting as we do.

NOTE FROM THE PUBLISHER

The information presented is true and complete to the best of our knowledge. All recommendations are made without any guarantees on the part of the author or the publisher, who also disclaim all liability incurred with the use of this information.

TRADEMARKS

We recognize that some words, model names and designations, for example, mentioned herein are the property of the trademark holder. We use them for identification purposes only. This is not an official publication.

INFORMATION ON THE USE OF THIS PUBLICATION

This manual is an invaluable resource for those interested in performing their own maintenance. However, in today's information age we are constantly subject to changes in common practice, new technology, availability of improved materials and increased awareness of chemical toxicity. As such, it is advised that the user consult with an experienced professional prior to undertaking any procedure described herein. While every care has been taken to ensure correctness of information, it is obviously not possible to guarantee complete freedom from errors or omissions or to accept liability arising from such errors or omissions. Therefore, any individual that uses the information contained within, or elects to perform or participate in do-it-yourself repairs or modifications acknowledges that there is a risk factor involved and that the publisher or its associates cannot be held responsible for personal injury or property damage resulting from the use of the information or the outcome of such procedures.

WARNING!

One final word of advice, this publication is intended to be used as a reference guide, and when in doubt the reader should consult with a qualified technician.

THE BOOK OF 1930's BRITISH MOTORCYCLE GEARBOXES AND CLUTCHES

CONTENTS

NOTES

The predominance of the data included in this publication was compiled from 1924-1939 service documentation. However, much of that same information is applicable to motorcycles manufactured before and after those dates. For instance, gearboxes manufactured by Albion, Sturmey Archer, Burman, etc. were installed in a variety of earlier and later motorcycles. In addition, many of the motorcycle manufacturers also utilized their proprietary gearbox and clutch systems in both earlier and later models.

This publication also includes a complete listing of titles in the Motorcyclist's Library series. Many of those books expand on the repair and maintenance procedures for other mechanical and electrical components and will be of assistance to owners and restorers of classic, vintage and veteran motorcycles.

ALBION GEARBOXES
REPAIRS AND ADJUSTMENTS

By F. A. Coney

Fig. 1.—Dismantling the Clutch.
Note position of large and small rubbers relative to studs.
A. Clutch stud.   B. Small rubber.   C. Large rubber.   D. Clutch centre.

MODEL "H" FOUR-SPEED

WE will begin our description of the dismantling, repair and assembly of the Albion gearboxes with the four-speed, model "H." It is understood that the gearbox has been washed free from grease and dirt before starting to dismantle. The first operation is to remove the clutch, and this is done in the following manner.

DISMANTLING

Dismantling the Clutch

Unscrew the small pin in the middle of the disk on the clutch cap, this releases the disk which is there to prevent the three hexagon-headed screws from turning. Unscrew the three screws (all threads are right-hand, that is, are unscrewed in an anti-clockwise direction unless otherwise stated), which allow the cap to be taken off, followed by the clutch

1

springs and distance tubes from over the clutch studs and the outer or front clutch plate. This exposes a smaller plate which fits on the clutch studs, and is known as the

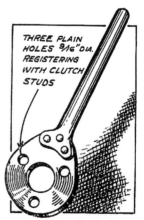

Fig. 2.—Tool for HOLDING CLUTCH WHILE UNSCREWING NUT.

rubber - retaining washer. This washer is drawn off, leaving a free passage for the steel friction disks, cork plates and sprocket to be withdrawn, and at the same time shows the rubber shock absorbers

Fig. 3.—REMOVING A DIFFICULT NUT.

This shows how to use the tool illustrated in Fig. 2 for holding clutch centre still whilst the nut is being unscrewed.

and clutch centre, together with the nut holding the centre on to the mainshaft (see Fig. 1).

Overcoming the First Difficulty

The removal of this nut presents a certain amount of difficulty ; in a service depot a special

Fig. 4.—Tool for WITHDRAWING CLUTCH.

Fig. 5.—Using the Clutch Withdrawal Tool.

tool is used for this (see Fig. 2). Failing this tool, wrap an odd length of chain round the final drive sprocket until it overlaps, and secure the end firmly; engage one of the gears, and then unscrew the nut anti-clockwise (see Fig. 3).

Two Methods of removing the Clutch Body

The clutch body is secured to the mainshaft by means of splines, and can usually be moved by jarring the end of the spindle with a brass hammer (do not use a steel hammer, as this will most certainly damage the thread). Assistance may be given by placing the curved ends of tyre levers at the back of the plate and levering gently. The best method, however, of withdrawing the clutch body is to use a tool after the de-scription of a sprocket drawer (see Fig. 4). This is made in the following manner. Obtain a steel disk about $2\frac{1}{4}$ inches diameter and $\frac{1}{4}$ inch thick, three $\frac{1}{4} \times 26$-inch thread pins and a $\frac{1}{2}$-inch bolt about 2 inches long ; drill three $\frac{3}{32}$-inch diameter holes in the disk to correspond with the holes in the clutch studs, and in the centre of the plate drill and tap a $\frac{1}{2}$-inch hole to suit the bolt. Place the disk on the clutch studs, and lock the three pins in the holes in the studs. Now screw the $\frac{1}{2}$-inch bolt through until it touches the end of the spindle. Further screwing of the bolt will draw the back plate off the mainshaft (see Fig. 5).

At the Other End of the Mainshaft

Attention is now directed for a few moments to the kick-starter end of the box. Remove the two bolts holding the bearing cap (see Fig. 6),

3

and take off cap complete with clutch lever. This exposes a nut on the end of the mainshaft, which has a left-hand thread, and consequently must be unscrewed in a clockwise direction. To unscrew this, retain the chain in position on the final drive sprocket, the end firmly held; have one of the gears engaged and unscrew nut (see Fig. 7).

Fig. 6.—DEALING WITH THE KICK-STARTER END OF THE GEARBOX.

This shows the bearing cap bolts referred to in the text.

Detaching Countershaft Sprocket

The final drive sprocket is splined on to the mainshaft sleeve and held there by means of a keyed washer and lock ring. The lock ring has three slots cut in the outside diameter, into which has been forced part of the key washer to prevent the ring from turning (see Fig. 8). First obtain a flat-nosed punch, and tap in the slots to flatten the key washer. Retain the chain round the sprocket and, using the same square punch, tap the lock ring round, anti-clockwise, to unscrew it (see Fig. 9). When this is clear the washer and sprocket can be pulled off. Sometimes there is a thin washer or shim between the end of the boss on the final drive sprocket and the ballrace against which it abuts. Note carefully if there is one, and if so, replace it when assembling.

4

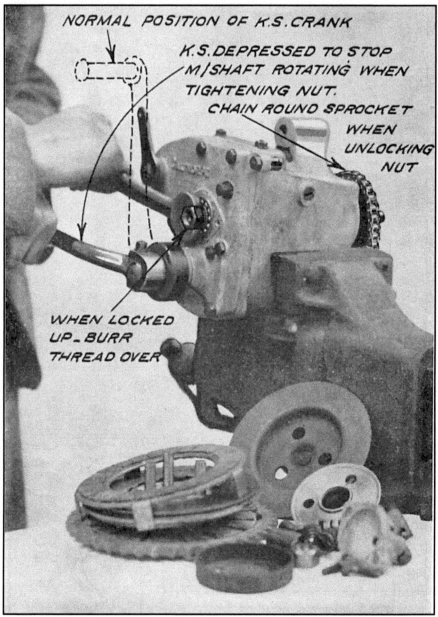

Fig. 7.—THIS SHOWS MORE ACCURATELY THE LOCKING UP OF THE NUT, USING THE KICK-STARTER CRANK TO KEEP SHAFT STILL.

To remove nut, chain should be held round final drive sprocket.

SQUARE NOSED
PUNCH

CHAIN
FIRMLY HELD
TO PREVENT
SPROCKET
TURNING

WASHER FORCED INTO SLOTS
IN LOCK
RING.   CHISEL

Fig. 9.—REMOVING THE BACK RING.
Note how the chain is being used to hold
the sprocket still.

Fig. 8.—WASHER DRIVEN INTO
SLOTS OF LOCK RING.

Another Useful Tool

A tool for unscrewing the lock ring can be made with a piece of steel tube, in the end of which are cut three dogs to correspond with the slots in the lock ring, and at the other end of the tube is drilled a hole to take a tommy bar (see Fig. 10). If driving round with a square punch, care must be taken not to swell the lock ring, otherwise when replaced it will not fit flat (see Fig. 11).

If the Kick-starter is Difficult to Remove

The kick-starter crank may now be removed by unscrewing the nut on the cotter pin and giving the threaded end of the cotter pin a sharp tap with a brass hammer to loosen it and allow it to be withdrawn. The crank will now pull off unless the cotter slot on the shaft is burred over, which is due to allowing the cotter pin to become loose, and if this is so the crank must be left in position for awhile. The plunger box should now be unscrewed from the cover; this is in the cover face and looks like a cover bolt, except that it has a collar below the hexagon. Inside the plunger box will be found a plunger and spring (see Fig. 12); if they do not come out with the box, look for them immediately the gearbox is opened, as otherwise they may get lost. The cover bolts can now be taken out and cover lifted off complete with kick-starter mechanism. Do not use a screwdriver or similar tool to prise the cover off, as this will tend to destroy the joint and cause oil leaks; a few light taps on the back of the operator box and the clutch end of the mainshaft will loosen it sufficiently to allow it to be drawn off. If the crank could not be removed, the end of the shaft just showing through the crank (Fig. 13) should be tapped to free, meanwhile holding the crank firmly on something solid. When the crank is removed, smooth the shaft by the cotter slot, where marks will be seen showing the digging in of the cotter pin. When

TOMMY BAR
TUBE
THREE DOGS TO FIT LOCK RING

Fig. 10.—TOOL FOR REMOVING LOCK RING.

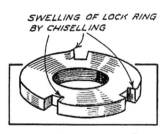

SWELLING OF LOCK RING BY CHISELLING

Fig. 11.—SWELLING OF LOCK RING.

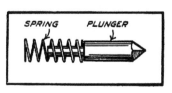

SPRING PLUNGER

Fig. 12.—THE PLUNGER AND SPRING.

These are contained in the plunger box indicated in Fig. 6. Take care they are not lost when the gearbox is dismantled.

this is done, the kick-starter shaft can be pushed out of the cover. Take off the steel plate on the back of the operator by removing the two holding screws, and the operator shaft and lever can then be taken out (see Fig. 14).

Rebushing the Kick-starter Bearing

The kick-starter shaft consists of the

Fig. 13.—To REMOVE KICK-STARTER CRANK. Tapping the end of the shaft to free the crank.

main body, inside which is a phosphor-bronze bush. If this bush is worn the shaft must be returned to the works for renewal, as special tools are necessary to withdraw the old bush and insert and ream the new one to size.

The Kick-starter Pawl

Between the two flanges on the shaft is the kick-starter pawl, which pivots on a pin, and is held out by a spring directly under the broad part or nose of the pawl. The pin is pushed in from the open end

Fig. 14.—THE FINAL STAGE IN DISMANTLING THE KICK-STARTER.

A. Operator box.
B. Lever on operator shaft.
C. Screws securing operator cover plate.
D. Spoon of operator lever.
E. Kick-starter stop.
F. Nose of pawl.

of the shaft up to a shoulder and the end is burred over to retain it in position. In order to remove the pawl it is necessary first of all to grind off the burred-over portion and tap the pin out from the kick-starter crank end (see Fig. 15). When

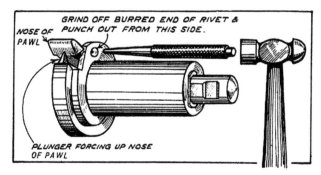

Fig. 15.—How to remove the Kick-starter Pawl.

the pin is nearly out, hold one finger over the pawl to prevent the spring from pushing it out and allowing it to fall and possibly get lost. The spring rests in the hole and is not retained in any way.

And Trip Plate

Inside the cover is a semicircular piece of steel with a hooked end (see Fig. 16). This is the kick-starter stop and trip plate, and it is held in position by means of two screws, the heads of which are on the outside of the cover. The plate will not fall out when the pins are removed owing to the fact that it is a light press fit at each end in the cover, but with a little levering it will come out quite easily.

Withdrawing the Gears

The cover is now stripped, and this leaves us with the gearbox and gears. The mainshaft is withdrawn complete with oil thrower—a round disk with a worm thread cut on the outside—a small gear and dog. Do not attempt to remove these latter two if either is broken, as the shaft must be returned to the works so that the new gear or dog, whichever is necessary, can be put on dead true. Just jutting outside the open end of the box at the top is a small ball-shaped end of a lever; push this to the right (see Fig. 17), and it will bring the sliding gears towards the open end of the box. Grasp the layshaft and mainshaft sliding gears with the fork between them, and draw the whole as a block out of the gearbox. The mainshaft sleeve and large low-gear pinion can now be taken out, leaving inside the box only the inside operator and bearings. The inside operator is held at the top and bottom by anchor pins (see Fig. 18). The anchor pins have screwdriver slots in their

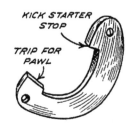

Fig. 16.—Kick-starter Stop and Trip Plate.

Fig. 17.—WITHDRAWING THE GEARS.

Note how the upper end of the lever A is being raised by the thumb.

A. Operator lever.   B. Long flat on fork towards mainshaft.   C. Layshaft.

heads, into which a little aluminium of the case has been driven to prevent their turning (see Fig. 19). This must be chipped out and the screws withdrawn, and this will allow the operator to be taken out. The box is now stripped down, and everything should be washed in paraffin for examination.

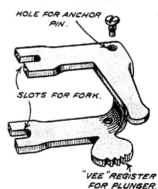

Fig. 18.—INSIDE OPERATOR.

INSPECTION AND REPAIR

Attention to Bushes and Bearings

If the main ballrace has worn, it should be driven out from the clutch end (see Fig. 20) and a new one inserted. This should be caulked

Fig. 19.—ALUMINIUM IN ANCHOR-PIN HEADS.

in by giving the aluminium immediately round it a blow with the chisel to force a little in round the radius, thus holding the bearing firmly (see Fig. 21). If the brushes are worn in the cover or box, no attempt should be made to renew them; they should be sent back to the service depot, as they have to be inserted correctly and reamed in a jig to get the correct diameter and alignment (as bushes are a press fit they contract a little, and cannot therefore be sent out to the correct size).

What to look for in the Layshaft Assembly

The layshaft assembly consists of the shaft, the large kick-starter pinion which is pressed on splines, two sliding pinions and the small low-gear pinion followed by a steel bush. Any replacements necessary for this shaft require the shaft to be sent complete to the works, because, as pointed out when dealing with the mainshaft, the fitting of new pinions necessitates great care to get the correct line. The small dogs on the layshaft are rounded, and the dogs on the sliding gears, which are internal dogs, are rounded to fit. If the gears have been jumping out of second and third, look at the dogs on the sliding gears, and if they are rounded outwards (see Fig. 22) the shaft should be returned to the works to have the gears replaced.

Fig. 20. — DRIVING WORN MAIN BALL-RACE OUT FROM CLUTCH END.

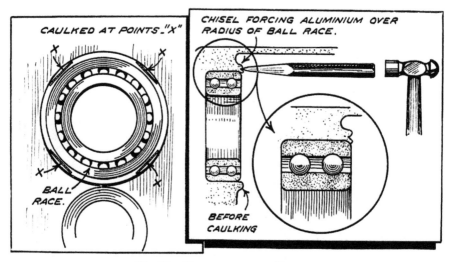

Fig. 21.—CAULKING IN THE BEARING.

Check the Inside Operator

Troubles do not arise much from the inside operator, the bow-shaped steel strip, with an arm terminating in a ball shape at one end and at the top extension, and on the lower extension a flat piece of steel, in which notches are cut (see Fig. 18). If the gears have been forced at any time, for instance when the machine has been standing stationary, then look in the neck of the ball to see if there are any cracks ; if there are, replace it immediately. The notches are the registrations for gears into which the plunger fits.

A Little Dentistry

The large gear on the mainshaft sleeve and also the mainshaft sliding gear should be examined for rounded dogs ; if these exist (see Fig. 23), they should be replaced, as they will cause gears to jump out. If a tooth has been broken off any of the gears, careful search should be made for it in order to prevent it remaining in the box and getting mixed up with other gears, thereby causing other breakages.

Check Shafts for Truth

The shafts should, if possible, be examined for truth by means of centres (see Fig. 24). The shaft should be placed between the centres and spun slowly against a white background. If the shaft moves up and down it is bent slightly, and should be returned to the works for straightening. Bending of the shafts is usually due to a tooth breaking off and getting between two other gears, forcing them apart. If no centres are

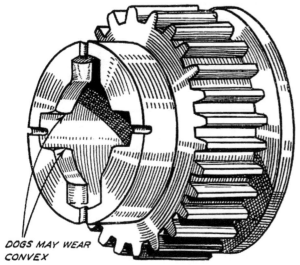

ROUNDED INSTEAD
OF SHARP CORNERS

Fig. 23.—ROUNDING OF
DOGS ON PINIONS.

DOGS MAY WEAR
CONVEX

Fig. 22.—ROUNDING OF DOGS IN SLIDING GEAR.

available, a rough-and-ready method is to place a straightedge (one that IS straight) along the shaft in three or four positions round the diameter, and holding it up to the light to see if there is any bending taking place (see Fig. 25).

The Need for Precision

The mainshaft should now be measured for wear by means of a micrometer. The diameter should not be more than ·006 inch below the nearest nominal size above, and assuming that the shaft in question measures ·806 inch, the obvious nominal size above is $\frac{13}{16}$ — ·8125 inch. The shaft is therefore ·0065 inch below and getting near to renewal time. Excessive clearance between the shaft and sleeve causes oscillation and oil leaks. There should not be more than ·010 inch between the shaft and the sleeve (see Fig. 26). This can be measured by means of a feeler gauge. This ·010 inch is, of course, considerably magnified at the clutch, when this is gripped and rocked. At the clutch end of the spindle will be seen the splines on which the clutch body is secured ; these should

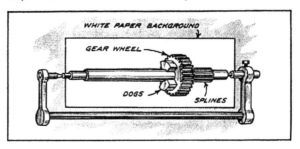

WHITE PAPER BACKGROUND

GEAR WHEEL

DOGS

SPLINES

Fig. 24.—MAINSHAFT IN CENTRES.

be examined because, if for some reason the nut holding the clutch has worked loose, the clutch body will probably have crept a little, rocked and worn the splines, possibly distorting them. If the clutch body can

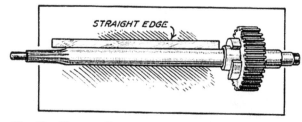

Fig. 25.—TESTING SHAFT FOR TRUTH WITH STRAIGHTEDGE.
Place the straightedge along the shaft in three or four positions round the diameter. Any bending will be apparent if the shaft is held up to the light at each position.

be assembled on them and locked up so that it is absolutely rigid, then all will be well, as long as it is kept rigid, but if it cannot be locked solid, or if it works loose quickly, a new shaft is indicated.

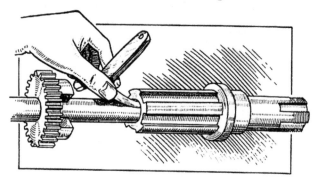

Fig. 26.—CLEARANCE BETWEEN SHAFT AND SLEEVE.

Examine the Fork

The fork between the sliding gears should be examined, but little trouble is anticipated here owing to the fact that it is not really heavily stressed. The only troubles will be due to wear on the pegs and the blades actually in contact with the gears. If the box has seen a lot of use, and there is an appreciable amount of wear, the fork should be replaced (see Fig. 27).

Should the Pawl be Replaced?

This leaves us with the cover assembly to deal with. We have already dealt with the bush in the kick-starter shaft, which brings us to the pawl. If the spring under the pawl has been jamming or is broken, the pawl will not have been held up to its work, and the nose will be burred over very badly, due to the fact that it has not been pushed right home into the teeth of the kick-starter pinion. In this case it must be renewed. If, however,

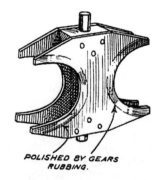

POLISHED BY GEARS RUBBING.

Fig. 27.—FORK, SHOWING PEGS AND BLADES, WHICH SHOULD BE EXAMINED FOR WEAR.

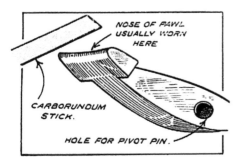

Fig. 28.—If Nose of Pawl is only Slightly Burred Over, reshape it with a Carborundum Stick.

it is only slightly burred over, it can be brought to its original shape by touching up with a carborundum stick (see Fig. 28).

Fitting the Pawl

If the spring has been jamming, but is not broken, then cleaning the hole out will cure this. To assemble, place the spring in the hole, followed by pawl plunger, then the pawl in position, and push the pivot pin through from the open end of the shaft, small diameter first, as far as it will go, and rivet the small end over. A useful sort of anvil on which to hold the one end of the pin is a ¼-inch ball or a piece of ¼-inch round steel (see Fig. 29).

Check the Kick-starter Shaft

At the end of the kick-starter shaft is cut a slot into which the cotter pin fits (see Fig. 30). If this is badly worn, it means that the nut on the cotter pin has been allowed to work loose, and the pin has slacked off, with the result that the wedging action has been lost, and as the kick-starter crank has been depressed to start the engine, a little

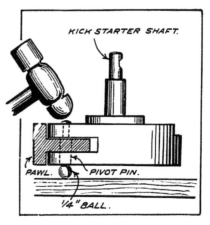

Fig. 29.—Riveting Pivot Pin for Pawl.

Note the ball, which is used as an anvil.

play has been allowed. This rapidly grows, and the cotter pin gradually cuts its way into the shaft, thereby spoiling both shaft and cotter pin. If the shaft is badly worn, a new one is necessary, but if it is not too badly worn the swelling should be taken out with a file.

Refitting the Trip Plate

The kick-starter stop and trip plate should be examined to see if it is swelled at all at the hook end (see Fig. 31); if so, it

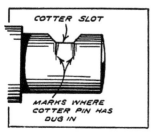

Fig. 30.—Wear on Kick-starter Shaft.

Caused through loose cotter pin.

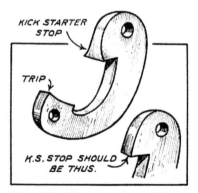

Fig. 31.—Swelling on Kick-starter Stop and Trip Plate.

should be smoothed off by rubbing with a stick of carborundum, after which it may be replaced by fitting into the cover and tapping gently down until it is flat on the two bosses supporting it; the bolts should now be screwed in and locked tightly.

Test Kick-starter Shaft Bearing

The kick-starter shaft should now be inserted into its bush and tested for play. There should be no more than is necessary to allow it to turn. Much clearance here will allow a slight oil leak; this, though not serious, is unsightly, especially as in many cases the exhaust pipe is under the shaft.

Very Important Check

In the top part of the cover is the operator shaft and lever. This consists of a spoon-shaped lever (see Fig 32) welded on to a round shaft, which is squared on the outside to accommodate the gearbox lever. The bush should be tested for play, only a few thousandths being permissible, and if a new one is necessary, unless in the hands of a competent man, it should be returned to works for exchange. The lever and shaft should be absolutely solid, and if there is any movement between them they must be replaced.

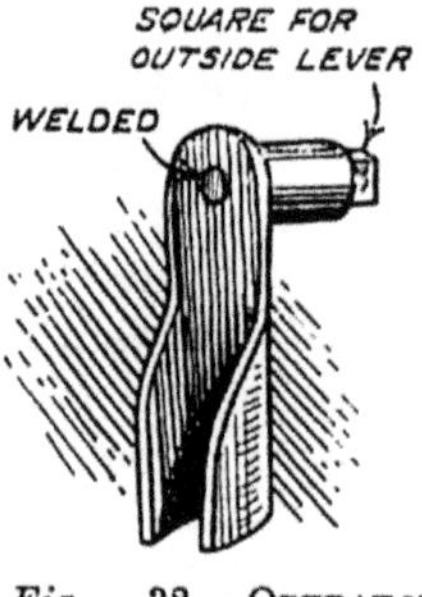

Fig. 32.—Operator Shaft and Lever.

If the Clutch is Difficult to Operate

In the clutch lever will be found a short hardened screw locked in position by a nut. The nose of the screw is polished and ground (see Fig. 33); if the nose has any flats worn on it, it must be exchanged, as this small pin presses against the push rod when declutching, and unevenness on the surface of the pin or the push rod will make the clutch difficult to operate. If the push rod has a small round hollow in the end, it should be ground square and flat (see Fig. 33).

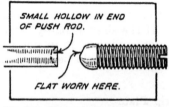

Fig. 33.—Wear at End of Clutch Push Rod and Pin.

End of push rod should be ground flat and the pin renewed.

Where to look for Cracks

In the case of a gearbox of the top fixing type, that is, with the studs on the top of the box, it may have had a knock whilst traversing rough roads. The shell should therefore be examined for cracks, and if any are seen a new case is the best remedy. Welding will mend a crack, but unfortunately the heat causes distortion.

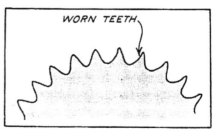

Fig. 34.—WEAR ON SPROCKETS.
Distinguished by the hook-like appearance of the teeth.

Attention to the Sprockets

That completes the box and cover, and attention must now be paid to the clutch and sprockets. If the sprockets are showing distinct signs of hooking (see Fig. 34), they should be replaced, as this hooking will rapidly ruin a chain. If the sprockets are wearing away badly down one side only of the teeth (see Fig. 36), then look to the chain alignment, as this wear shows that it is not running square and true with its corresponding sprocket. If the sprockets are worn down quite regularly, they must, of course, be renewed.

How to Recork the Clutch Plates

The clutch is built up of cork inserts which will wear many thousands of miles if treated properly, that is, not slipped. If the corks in either the sprocket or any of the intermediate plates show signs of " charring " or are brittle and " chippy," have them recorked, and look to the clutch adjustment when putting the box back on the machine. It is quite easy to put new corks in a sprocket or plate ; soak them for a few minutes in boiling water and they will become pliable ; they should then be pushed into the holes, the edges tucked in with a screwdriver, and the faces tapped as flat and level as possible (see Fig. 38). It is far better to return them to the works to be corked, so that they can be ground to their correct thickness.

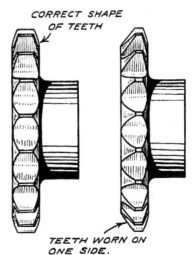

CORRECT SHAPE OF TEETH

TEETH WORN ON ONE SIDE.

Figs. 35 and 36.—EFFECT ON SPROCKETS OF CHAIN OUT OF LINE.

The Shock Absorbers

The rubbers should now be inspected, but these again last many miles, but since they perform a very important function, namely, that of absorbing the shocks transmitted from the engine, they should be replaced when the edges start to fray and pile up against the retaining washer.

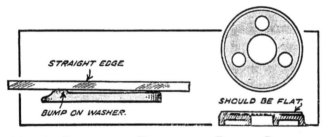

The retaining washer should be checked by placing a straightedge across its surface in several places to ascertain whether it is dead flat or not (see

Fig. 37.—TESTING FOR FLATNESS OF RUBBER RETAINING WASHER. USING A STRAIGHTEDGE.

Shows how unevenness is discovered.

Fig. 37). If it has buckled it will allow a certain amount of play on the clutch unit, and consequently should be replaced.

Studs and Springs

If a clutch stud has to be replaced it should be returned to the works, as after riveting it must

Fig. 38.—RECORKING THE CLUTCH PLATES.

Soak the corks in boiling water for a few minutes, push into holes and tuck into edges with a screwdriver. The faces must afterwards be ground level.

be recessed true to the clutch body. Lastly come the springs; in due course these are bound to lose some of their resiliency, and as a test two should be placed in a vice end to end with a strip of flat steel between them and the vice gradually tightened. Care must be taken that they are dead square and opposite each other, or they may fly up and do the operator some facial injury. If one close-coils, that is,

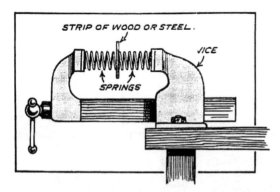

Fig. 39.—HOW TO TEST SPRINGS FOR WEAKNESS.

Weakness of spring is indicated when one coil binds or closes before the other.

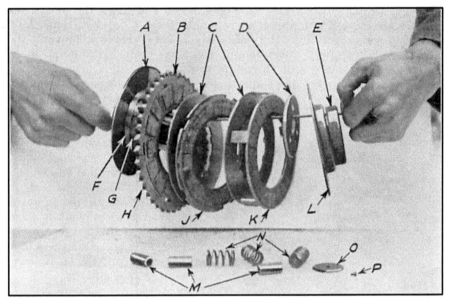

Fig. 40.—Clutch Parts showing Order of Assembly.

A. Back plate.	F. Ball ring.	L. Front plate.
B. Clutch studs.	G. Drum containing shock absorber.	M. Distance tubes.
C. Steel intermediate plates.	H. Sprocket.	N. Springs.
D. Rubber retaining washer.	J. Grooved cork plate.	O. Clutch cap plate.
E. Clutch cap.	K. Tongued cork plate.	P. Centre screw.

the coils touch one another sooner than the other, it means that its temper has gone somewhat; this indicates that the others are probably in the same state, and they should be replaced (see Fig. 39).

REASSEMBLY

The Order of Reassembly

Before commencing to assemble wash everything thoroughly in clean paraffin, and allow it to drain off, as paraffin is not a lubricant. The first operation is to fit the inside operator, take the operator anchor pins and screw them into the box until the nose is just

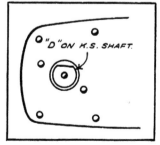

Fig. 41.—Showing the Flat on the Kick-starter Shaft.

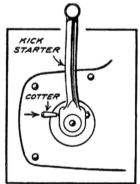

Fig. 42.—Note that the Cotter Pin holding the Kick-starter Crank must be inserted from the Left.

19

showing through, then slide the operator in and screw the pins home tightly, giving the aluminium surrounding them a tap with the chisel to drive some of it into the screwdriver slot; this will prevent the screws from turning. Next mount the large mainshaft pinion on to the mainshaft sleeve and thread it through the ball bearing, slip on the final drive sprocket, not forgetting to insert a small packing washer,

if there was one; tap it up the splines, place on the keyed washer and screw on the lock ring. Wrap the odd length of chain round the sprocket to prevent it from turning, secure the end and then lock up the lock ring deadtight.

An Important Precaution

As a further precaution a small chisel should be driven under the washer between the slots of the lock ring to drive some of the metal into the slots. Oil should now be run in to the layshaft bearing in the box, and the complete layshaft, together with the operating fork and the

Fig. 43.—DRIVING CLUTCH CENTRE ON TO MAINSHAFT.

mainshaft sliding gear in position, should be inserted as a block into the box. The inside operator should be swivelled so that the slots in the end of the arms face as near the open end of the box as possible and the pegs on the fork inserted in them; then with a little manœuvring the mainshaft slider will drop on the mainshaft sleeve, the smaller gear of the two being towards the open end of the box and the end of the layshaft will be introduced into its bush. It will probably be necessary to rotate the layshaft a little in order to allow the teeth on the small gear to mesh with the corresponding teeth on the large pinion on the mainshaft sleeve.

Oil Preferred to Grease

More oil should now be poured in, taking care that the shafts and gears are well covered. We do not advise grease for this box, as it chokes the oilways and leads to seizures ; a little *very light* grease may be used to have a retarding effect on the gears when the clutch is released. The mainshaft should now be well covered with oil and inserted in the sleeve, the teeth of the pinion mounted on it meshing with the kick-starter wheel on the layshaft. This is followed by the oil thrower and packing shim, if any.

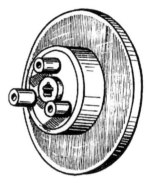

Fig. 44.—Solid ·Type of Back Plate.

Assembling the Cover

Leaving the box for awhile, the cover is to be assembled. Place the operator lever in position, and fix the cover by means of the two securing pins ; the kick-starter shaft should now be inserted in its bush and turned in a clockwise direction (looking at the outside of the cover) until the stop

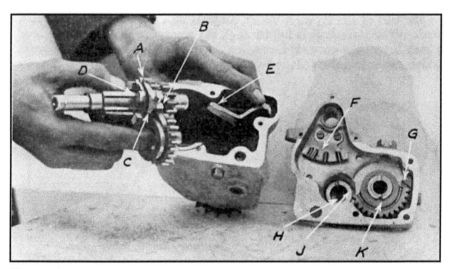

Fig. 45.—Dismantling the Three-speed Model.

A. Layshaft slider.
B. Wide flat on fork faces mainshaft.
C. Bosses on fork.
D. Layshaft splines.
E. Note how this lever is being depressed

Fig. 46.—The Cover of the Three-speed Gearbox.

F. Locating plate.
G. Kick-starter stop pin.
H. Mainshaft adjusting nut.
J. Mainshaft adjusting bush.
K. Kick-starter segment.

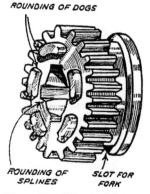

Fig. 47.—EXAMINING THE HIGH-GEAR PINION FOR WEAR ON DOGS.

Fig. 48.—EXAMINING THE SLIDING PINION FOR ROUNDING OF DOGS AND SPLINES.

on the segment shaft engages against the stop on the plate, when it can be turned no farther. It will be seen that the pawl has now been depressed through contact with the other end of the stop plate, which forms a trip (see Fig. 14).

Fitting the Cover

The gearbox cover is now ready for fitting to the box. Pour some oil on the end of the layshaft which projects into the bush in the segment shaft. The mainshaft is fed through the bearing in the cover, and about $\frac{1}{2}$ inch before the cover is home, see that the ball on the inside operator, which stands just clear of the box, enters the spoon portion of the operating

Fig. 49.—PRESSURE WASHER.

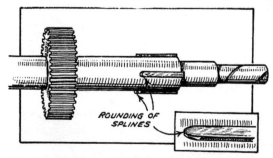

Fig. 50.—EXAMINING THE MAINSHAFT AND LAYSHAFT FOR ROUNDING OF THE SPLINES.

lever ; tap the cover gently down and insert the cover screws, one of which takes the loop on the kick-starter return spring (see Fig. 6). On the pivot type this is the one next below the plunger spring box, and on the top or bottom fixing types it is the one on the left-hand bottom corner, so this one should be left until last.

The Kick-starter Spring

Take the kick-starter spring and the cover and place it on the kick-starter shaft so that the flat of the " D " hole rests on the flat milled on the shaft (see Fig. 41). Holding this in position, thread the cover bolt which takes the loop through it, and bolt it in its correct hole. Now the kick-starter crank is to be placed on and the cotter pin inserted. The cotter pin is to be inserted from the left, so that when the crank is depressed the nut is on top (see Fig. 42). If placed in the reverse way the cotter pin will not stand much kick-starting ; drive the pin in hard and lock the nut tight.

The Mainshaft Nut is a Left-hand Thread

The mainshaft nut should now be screwed on, remembering that it is left hand and is screwed on in an anticlockwise direction. The mainshaft can be stopped from turning by depressing the kick-starter and holding it rigidly (see Fig. 7). When the nut is tight, tap the thread over a little to stop any chance of the nut unlocking.

How to fit the Gear Locating Plunger

Now take the plunger, spring and plunger box,

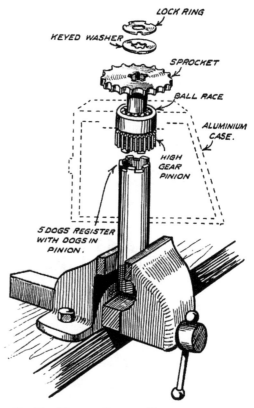

Fig. 51.—Using a Dogged Tool for holding the High-gear Pinion during Reassembly.

insert the plunger spring and plunger in the box, and see that they slide easily ; then proceed to screw it in. As soon as resistance is felt the plunger box should be rotated backwards and forwards a few times, and at the same time the gear moved ; this will ensure that the nose of the plunger fits square into the " Vee " of the register of the inside operator. Oil the bearing, and the bearing cap may be placed in position and the two holding screws screwed home.

Reassembling the Clutch

Put a little grease on the balls in the clutch sprocket, and then assemble the back clutch plate, sprocket, steel friction plate, grooved cork plate, steel friction plate and tanged cork plate in that order, making certain that the tangs on the cork plate pass through the grooves in the grooved plate and then through the slots in the sprocket (see Fig. 40). Place the body on the shaft, and tap it right home by means of a piece of tube in the recess of the clutch centre (see Fig. 43). Lock up the nut holding the body on to the mainshaft. Then place into position the rubber retaining plate, front clutch plate, distance tubes, clutch springs and cap, insert the three screws and screw them home tightly. Put on the small round disk, turning the hexagon heads of the pins slightly until it fits, and screw in the small centre pin.

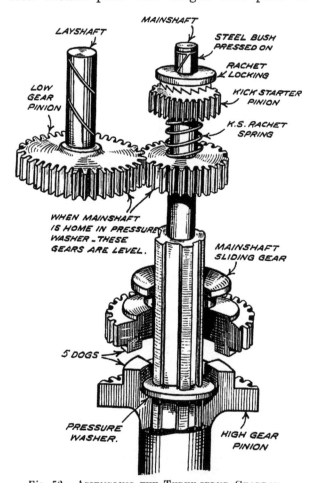

Fig. 52.—ASSEMBLING THE THREE-SPEED GEARBOX.

When the mainshaft is properly assembled, the low-gear pinion should be in line with the small pinion on the mainshaft as shown above.

THREE-SPEED MODELS

The range of three-speed boxes consist of Model " G " for 500 c.c., Model " J " for 350 c.c., and Model " E " up to 300 c.c. Many parts in the three-speed models are similar to parts in the four-speed, and the reader is recommended to read about the four-speed first, so that he will understand the reference " the same as in the four-speed." The three

three-speed models are alike in construction, with the exception of the clutch, and also in operation, so that the description of one will suffice for the whole range. The difference in clutches lies in the number of plates and the size: the " G " model and some " J " models have three plate

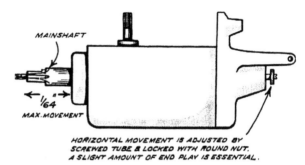

Fig. 53.—TAKING UP ENDPLAY ON THE MAINSHAFT.
The above adjustment should be made to bring the endplay down to $\frac{1}{64}$ inch.

clutches, some of the " J's " and some of the " E's " have two plate clutches, and the remaining " E's " have single plate clutches, and are used chiefly on the 175- and 196-c.c. engines.

The Difference between Shock Absorber and Solid Type

The clutch may be a shock absorber or solid type (see Fig. 44). If it is the shock-absorber type, then the same procedure follows in dismantling as on the four-speed, with the exception of course of the number of plates; the principle, however, is the same. With the solid type, dismantling is begun in the same way, but the difference is that there are no rubbers, no distance tubes and no drum; a solid centre with the studs riveted to the back plate takes the place of the drum, centre and rubbers.

Similar Methods used

The solid centre is drawn off the shaft in the same manner as the shock-absorber centre. The method used for removing the lock-ring, key washer and final-drive sprocket is the same as that used with the four-speed. Turning to the kick-starter end of the box, remove the plunger box complete with plunger and spring, then the cover bolts and lift off the cover.

Do not damage the Joint

We must emphasise the necessity for avoiding the use of a screwdriver or similar tool to prise off the cover. Tap on the back of the kick-starter crank, and this will free the cover, which may be stripped down in the following manner: remove the crank by withdrawing the cotter pin, take off the return spring and cover, and tap the shaft out of the cover. Inside the cover

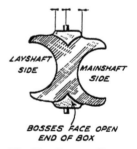

Fig. 54.—SPECIAL FORK FOR " E " AND " J " MODELS.

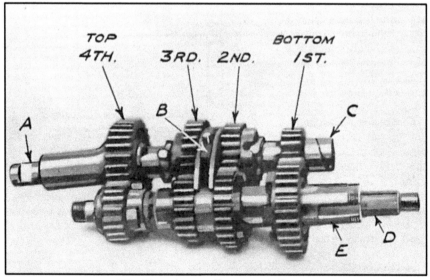

Fig. 55A.—ALBION FOUR-SPEED GEARS.

A. Kick-starter shaft.   C. Steel Bush.
B. Long Flat on Fork, towards Mainshaft.   D. Mainshaft.
                    E. Mainshaft Sleeve.

is a round-headed screw, against which the return spring forces the kick-starter segment; this is the kick-starter stop pin, and is a plain screw into the cover locked on the outside with a nut. Next remove the three pins holding the steel operator cover on the back of the operator box (see Fig. 46) and withdraw operator.

Withdrawing the Gears, etc.

Remove the mainshaft complete with pinion, kick-starter ratchet and spring, then take out the large gear pinion on the layshaft. Press the ball of the inside operator to the right as in the four-speed, and withdraw the layshaft with sliding pinion, fork and mainshaft sliding pinion as a block (see Fig. 45). The high-gear pinion may now be taken out, noting that in a recess slightly larger than the hole through which the spindle passes is a washer in which is a hole shaped to fit the splines (see Fig. 49). This leaves the inside operator and bearings in the shell. The inside operator is removed in the same manner as the four-speed, which it strongly resembles, by chipping out the aluminium from the slots in the anchor pins and unscrewing them.

Careful Examination Needed

Everything should be carefully washed in paraffin before examination. All phosphor-bronze bearings which are worn should be returned to the

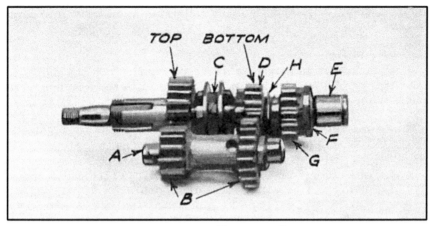

Fig. 55B.—ALBION TWO-SPEED GEARS.

A. Layshaft.
B. Layshaft gears.
C. Dog clutch.
D. Low-gear pinion.

E. Steel bush.
F. Kick-starter lock nut.
G. Kick-starter ratchet pinion.
H. Spring washer.

works for renewal, owing to the fact that they must be reamed to size and in correct line. The high-gear pinion should be examined for wear on the dogs (see Fig. 47), or wear in the bore ; this may be tested by using a feeler gauge in conjunction with the insertion on the spindle. The clearance here should not exceed ·010 to ·012 inch.

Cause of Gear jumping out

The sliding pinion should be inspected for rounding of the dogs and the hole for rounding of the splines (see Fig. 48). If the middle gear has been jumping out this will probably be found to be the cause. The dogs on the large pinion on the layshaft should be inspected for wear. The layshaft has a small top-gear pinion splined on, and this is followed by a steel bush also pressed on splines. If any renewals are required the shaft should be returned to the works in order that the parts may be pressed on correctly and the diameter of the bush made true with the shaft. The foregoing remarks apply also to the mainshaft, which has a small pinion pressed on, followed by the kick-starter pinion, which is free to slide against the spring, followed by a steel bush.

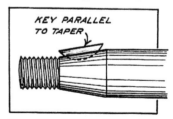

Check Ratchets

The condition of the ratchet on both pinions of the mainshaft should be noted,

Fig. 56.—ILLUSTRATING THE METHOD OF SECURING THE CLUTCH CENTRE ON TWO-SPEED MODELS.

and if either set of ratchets is badly chipped it would be well to renew the part.

Also both Shafts

Both mainshaft and layshaft should be examined on the splines for rounding (see Fig. 50), as this, in conjunction with the rounding of the splines in the sliding gears, will cause trouble in holding middle gear.

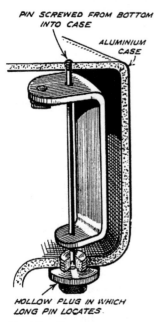

PIN SCREWED FROM BOTTOM INTO CASE

ALUMINIUM CASE

HOLLOW PLUG IN WHICH LONG PIN LOCATES.

Fig. 57.—Dismantling the Two-speed Model.

The inside operator cannot be removed until the hollow plug shown above has been unscrewed.

Special Attention to Kick-starter Segment

The kick-starter segment is pressed on to splines on the kick-starter shaft, and the splines are riveted over at the end to secure the segment in position. If the segment requires renewing, the shaft should be returned complete to the works for renewal.

How to test Bushes

The same remarks apply to the renewing of the phosphor-bronze bush in the shaft as in the four-speed: return it to the works. The bushes in the cover should be tested for play by inserting their respective shafts and rocking. In the end of the bush in which the mainshaft turns is screwed a hardened steel tube which is locked with a small round nut. This is used to provide end clearance correctly for the mainshaft, and should be slacked off before assembly. The examination of the operating lever and the round-nosed screw in the clutch lever concludes the inspection.

REASSEMBLING THREE-SPEED MODELS

The assembly of this pattern commences with the insertion of the high-gear pinion in the ballrace, and mounting on it the final-drive sprocket, lock ring and keyed washer. The chain may be wrapped round the sprocket to hold it whilst screwing the lock ring tight. Another way of holding the sprocket with this type is to obtain a dogged tool, and to insert it in the dogs of the high-gear pinion and then to screw on the lock ring in its position behind the final-drive sprocket, as shown in Fig. 51. Having locked the sprocket and lock ring in position, place the pressure washer in its recess in the the high-gear pinion. The inside operator should now be placed in the box, and the anchor pins screwed home, aluminium being driven into the slots in the head to prevent their turning.

Next press the ball on the operator to the right as in the four-speed; this brings the slots in its arms to the open end of the box; pour a little oil in the layshaft bush (see Fig. 45).

Insert the Gears together

Then take the layshaft, layshaft sliding gear and mainshaft sliding gear with the fork in between them, and pass them into the box, so that the pegs on the fork enter the slots in the arms of the operator; pass the gears farther in, and rotate the layshaft a little until the end is introduced into its bush in the box. A little hand pressure may be necessary to force this home, owing to the fact that the oil in the bush will form a buffer. The feel of this is easily distinguished from the feel of something solid, in which case no force should be used.

Rotate the shaft backwards and forwards, and the surplus oil will work out, allowing the shaft to go right home. The large pinion should now be oiled in the hole and placed on the layshaft, followed by the mainshaft being passed through the mainshaft slider and high-gear pinion. The mainshaft must be rotated and held lightly against the pressure washer in the high-gear pinion to ensure that the splines on the shaft fit in the grooves in the washer.

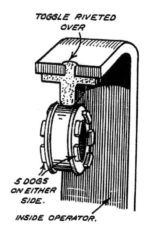

Fig. 58.—Showing how the Toggle is Secured in the Operator.

Check the Mainshaft

When the mainshaft is right home the teeth on the layshaft low-gear pinion will be in line with the teeth on the small pinion on the mainshaft (see Fig. 52).

Reassembling the Cover

The cover should now be assembled by inserting the operator lever in its bush, in which a little oil has been poured, and securing the triangular steel plate in position on the back of the operator box by means of the three screws. Oil the kick-starter shaft bearing, and push the kick-starter shaft in position; rotate in anti-clockwise direction, looking from the inside of the cover until the segment makes contact with the segment stop (see Fig. 46).

Fitting the Kick-starter

Now place the kick-starter return spring and the cover in position so that the " D " of the hole rests on the flat which is milled on the shaft, follow this with the kick-starter crank, which is secured by the cotter pin being driven tightly in and locked up with the nut and washer. Oil the bearing inside the kick-starter shaft, and also the bearing for the main shaft, the screwed tube in which should have been slacked off. Oil can now be poured in the gearbox, noting that it runs down the shafts, and the cover placed on the box.

Set the Operator Lever

About ⅛ inch before the cover is finally home see that the operator lever is moved to enclose in its spoon portion the ball of the inside operator. Insert the cover bolts and plunger box and lock down.

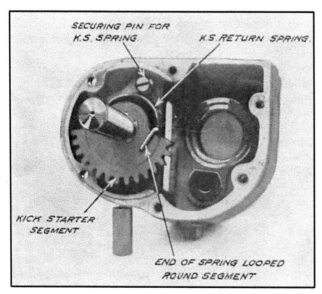

Fig. 59.—Reassembling the Two-speed Gearbox.
This shows how the kick-starter spring and segment are assembled.

How to take up End-play on Mainshaft

The mainshaft should now be tested for end-play, of which not more than $\frac{1}{64}$ inch should exist; any more should be taken up by means of the screwed tube in the mainshaft bearing. The tube is screwed in until it makes contact with the end of the main-shaft and is then withdrawn $\frac{1}{64}$ inch and locked down with the round nut so that end-play is just perceptible (see Fig. 53).

Examine Push-rod Screw

The round-nosed screw in the clutch lever should be examined for flats, and any small hollow in the push rod should be ground off; the clutch is built up and secured to the mainshaft in the same manner as in the four-speed.

Special Note for " E " and " J " Models

When assembling an " E " or " J " model, it should be noted that the layshaft is higher than the mainshaft, and that the fork between them, which moves the sliding gears, is made with one radius higher than the other : the high side takes the layshaft ; also the flat to one side of the peg is larger than the other : this side goes towards the mainshaft.

Part of the fork has been turned off, leaving a portion immediately below each peg on one face standing out. This side faces the open end of the box (see Fig. 54). When the control is fitted direct on the box a small plate is fitted inside the operator box, in the slots of which the "V" piece on the back of the operating lever fits. This is held by two small screws, and is there to prevent the long gear lever from oscillating (see Fig. 46).

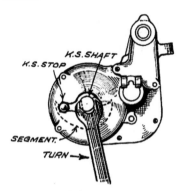

Fig. 60.—ANOTHER STAGE IN ASSEMBLING THE KICK-STARTER.

Turn the kick-starter shaft by means of a spanner as shown to bring the segment clear of the stop.

TWO-SPEED MODELS

The two-speed gearbox model "C" is used only on small machines with engines up to 150 c.c. The clutch is of the single plate solid type, as used on some of the "E" models; the only difference is that, instead of the centre being mounted on splines, it is on a taper, in which is a half-moon key (see Fig. 56).

Clutch Dismantling

The same procedure is followed in dismantling the clutch as in other models, and this applies also to the final-drive sprocket.

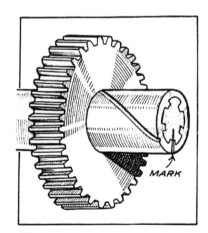

Fig. 61.—SHOWING HOW THE STEEL BUSH AND SHAFT SHOULD BE MARKED BEFORE DISMANTLING TO ENSURE THAT THEY CAN BE RE-ASSEMBLED CORRECTLY.

Remove Kick-starter and Cover

Next remove the kick-starter crank by withdrawing the cotter pin, and examine the shaft to see whether it is swelled or cut up by the cotter pin, and, if so, smooth it round with a file to its original diameter. Remove the cover bolts (there is no plunger or plunger box in this model), and pull off the cover, tapping the end of the kick-starter shaft to leave segment in position in the box. The operator lever should be examined by withdrawing the three screws holding the cover: this lever is the same as on all models. Behind the operator lever is a small spring plate which acts as a register for the gears, and is held in position by two small screws (see

31

Fig. 45). This plate is the same as the three-speed, except that it has three notches instead of four. The mainshaft adjusting screw (the screwed tube in the mainshaft bush) should be slacked off to ease assembly later.

How Layshaft is Removed

The spindle on which the layshaft gears rotate is screwed tightly into the cover, right-hand thread ; to withdraw this it should be held tightly in a vice, preferably with lead faces to protect the bearing surface, and the cover tapped round with a hide hammer or mallet anticlockwise.

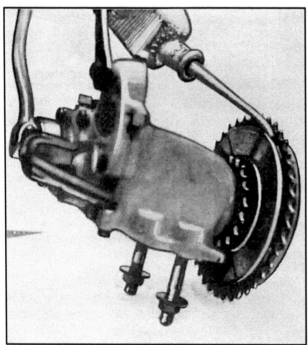

Fig. 62.—Oiling the Clutch.
Withdraw the clutch, and run oil down the sprocket between the corks on the dog plate side of the sprocket.

Kick-starter Segment

The kick-starter segment is returned by a spring, one end of which is anchored by a pin to the box while the other end is looped round the segment. The segment should be slipped out of the loop and withdrawn from its bush in the box. A small screw with a slotted head will be seen to hold the other end of the spring in a loop. This has a nut on the back of the kick-starter case, the removal of which allows the retaining pin to be unscrewed and the spring to be freed.

Extracting Mainshaft and Gears

The mainshaft may now be withdrawn, followed by the dog clutch and the layshaft gears and high-gear pinion, in which is the pressure washer. The inside operator is held in position by a long pin screwed into the top of the box from the bottom, and the bottom of the pin is located in a hollow screwed plug (see Fig. 57). The plug is removed first, right-hand thread, and this discloses the end of the long pin which

32

has a screwdriver slot, and is unscrewed out, right-hand thread. The inside operator may now be removed.

Fitting Layshaft Bush

The small steel bush in the box into which the layshaft fits is pressed in and dowel pegged. If it is necessary to renew this the dowel peg must be removed, the old bush knocked out, a new one inserted and drilled through the aluminium, tapped, and a new dowel peg inserted. After this it has to be reamed to size, so that unless the garage is well equipped it is a job that is better sent to the works. Any other bushes required must be sent with the part in which they fit, box or cover, to the service depot for replacement for reasons explained earlier.

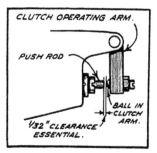

Inspecting Parts for Wear

The layshaft should be tested in the double gear for wear, and if necessary exchanged; ·010 to ·012 inch clearance is permissible, but above that wear will take place more rapidly, as the case hardening wears. Dogs on the high-gear pinion dog clutch, and on the low-gear dog-clutch pinion should be examined for rounding. The dog-clutch pinion is free to rotate on the mainshaft,

Fig. 63.—Illustrating the Correct Clearance between the Clutch Lever and Push Rod.

and is held in position by a pen-steel washer, a contracting spring washer and another pen-steel washer, which also acts as a stop for the ratchet spring. The spring holds the kick-starter ratchet pinion in mesh with the ratchet lock ring. A distance bush is placed on the shaft against the outside pen-steel washer, and it is on this bush that the ratchet pinion slides and rotates. The bush is held in position by the ratchet lock ring, which is pressed on splines on the shaft, followed by a steel bush, also pressed on. If any renewals are required on the shaft, it should be returned complete to the works. Test the spindle for wear in the high-gear pinion, not allowing more than about ·010 inch. In the inside operator will be found a small swivelling toggle which is riveted in. Should this be worn, it can be renewed by grinding off the riveted head, inserting a new one, and burring the head over (see Fig. 58), making certain that it swivels quite freely ; put a little oil on.

REASSEMBLING THE TWO-SPEED GEARBOX

The Gearbox

The examination is now complete, and the assembly can be commenced. Place the high-gear pinion through the ballrace and fit the

final-drive sprocket, keyed washer and lock ring, using chain to hold the
sprocket from turning, as described in the three- and four-speed models,
or the dogged tool as described in the three-speed assembly, if available.
Next thread the long operator pin through the hole in the bottom side
of the case, through the inside operator, screw it into the top of the
case and lock tightly. Follow this up with the hollow screwed plug, also
locked tightly. Place the pressure washer in the high-gear pinion, and
then engage the toggle between the flanges of the dog clutch and place
this on the high-gear pinion so that the dogs are in mesh (see Fig. 58).
Next insert the layshaft gears, small gear first, to mesh with the teeth of
the high-gear pinion. Oil the mainshaft, and pass it through the dog
clutch and high-gear pinion, rotating it either way until it drops home
through the pressure washer ; pour oil into the box, not omitting some in
the bore of the layshaft gears.

Replacing Kick-starter Spring

The kick-starter spring can now be replaced by threading the screwed
pin through the round loop of the spring, screwing it into the box and
locking up with a nut on the back. Place the kick-starter segment in its
bush in the box, and turn it to get the loop of the spring round the web of
the segment (see Fig. 59). Screw the layshaft into the cover absolutely
deadtight, and remove any marks on it caused by holding it when screwing or unscrewing by polishing with a very fine emery cloth. Place the
spring plate in position, securing it by the two pins, and follow this up
with the operating lever after oiling the bush and the steel cover. Put
some oil in the mainshaft and kick-starter shaft bearings, and place on
cover.

Adjust Operator Lever and Kick-starter Segment

Just before the cover is home see that the spoon of the operator lever
surrounds the ball of the inside operator, then turn the kick-starter shaft
anticlockwise for about one quarter turn to bring the segment clear of
the stop and the cover will drop into position (see Fig. 60). A little
manoeuvring may be necessary to get the end of the layshaft into the
small steel bush in the box. The cover now may be locked down by
the cover screws, and the kick-starter crank fitted with the cotter pin.

Refitting the Clutch

When fitting the clutch make certain that the tapers on the spindle
and in the clutch centre are perfectly dry and free from oil or grease :
rubbing them with chalk is a good drying medium. The key should be
inserted and tapped down, so that the top is parallel with the taper, and
the body knocked on tightly, followed by spring washer and nut. Build
up the clutch, as has been previously described.

ALBION GEARBOXES

Alterations in Later Models

At the end of 1928 the clutch on the three-speed models was altered to the ball-bearing type from a phosphor-bronze bearing. The stripping down is performed in exactly the same manner, the only difference being that instead of a steel drum, in the shock-absorber type, a phosphor-bronze drum was used, and in the solid type a phosphor-bronze ring on a steel centre was used instead of the hardened centre and balls.

Most Important

If the phosphor-bronze ring or drum is worn and requires renewing, the back plate complete must be returned to the works for refitting. In a well-equipped workshop changes of gears which are pressed on may be made, provided that before stripping down the steel bush is marked to show which spline fitted into its groove, and it must be replaced in *exactly* the same position, otherwise they almost certainly will not run true with the shaft (see Fig. 61).

GENERAL

Lubrication is very important: use engine oil, and pour in about $\frac{1}{4}$ pint every 2,000 miles. Lubricate all joints in controls to prevent wear and loss of gear registration. The clutch cable also should be lubricated occasionally. The sprocket bearing can be lubricated, and this applies particularly to the phosphor-bronze bearing type, which must be kept well lubricated, by declutching and running some oil down the sprocket between the corks on the back plate side of the sprocket (see Fig. 62). Do not strain gears by attempting to change when stationary.

Adjustments

There should be $\frac{1}{32}$ inch between the end of the push rod and the nose of the adjusting pin in the clutch lever (see Fig. 63). If there is any suspicion of clutch slip, look to the adjustment at this point. Unlock the nut and screw or unscrew the small pin to the correct distance and then lock the nut.

Chains

Use the correct size of chain for the sprocket; see that the chains are in line with the corresponding sprockets on the engine or rear wheel, and do not have the chains too tight. When sending for spares the letter and number on gearbox should be quoted, and patterns should be sent wherever possible to preclude the possibility of mistakes.

NOTES

OVERHAUL AND ADJUSTMENT OF THE VARIOUS B.S.A. CLUTCHES AND GEARBOXES

THE CLUTCH

The Clutch. This is of the floating dry-plate type. On the larger models it consists of seven friction rings and eight steel plates arranged alternately. There are thus fourteen bearing

Fig. 1. The B.S.A. Clutch Dismantled

surfaces with a total area of more than 200 sq. in.—an unusually large area for a motor-cycle clutch (Figs. 1 and 2). Every second steel plate is coupled by splines to the clutch drive which is driven by the primary chain. The other steel plates are splined to the clutch sleeve which is keyed on to the gearbox mainshaft. There are six clutch springs, and when the clutch is engaged these force the steel plates and friction rings together in such a way that the entire assembly rotates as a solid mass transmitting power from the engine shaft to the gearbox mainshaft. The large bearing area and effective diameter of the plates permit the use of medium strength springs.

FIG. 2.   THE B.S.A. PLATE CLUTCH

In the smaller models a lighter clutch of similar construction is fitted.

HEAVY - WEIGHT TYPE CLUTCH   (See Fig. 3.)

It is suggested that the clutch should be detached complete as one unit. The locking ring, with four slots, should then be unscrewed, preferably with a " Cee " spanner. To avoid stripping the last few threads it is advisable to take two long screws from the timing cover of the engine and screw these into the two holes in the thrust plate. When these are screwed home it will be noticed that the pressure is taken off the locking ring. With the locking ring off, the two screws can be removed and the plates lifted from the clutch chain wheel. If the clutch has been correctly assembled they should be taken out in the following order : outer or spring-thrust plate, plate holding the six springs and cups, fabric ring, lipped driving plate, fabric ring, then a driven plate (with six holes around the centre), fabric, lipped driving plate, fabric, driven, fabric, lipped, fabric, then the recessed driven plate, fabric, and finally the clutch chain wheel. *Note.*—The recessed centre of the last driven plate should be set outwards from the chain wheel, whilst the lipped plates should face inwards towards the wheel. There should therefore be seven fabric plates interposed between the steel ones.

The Clutch Chain-wheel Bearing

It is seldom necessary to dismantle the chain-wheel bearing, which consists of a double row of $\frac{1}{4}$-inch balls. Should it be necessary to adjust this, the locking washer should be removed and the cone unscrewed. *Note.*—This has a left-hand thread. The bearing can then be examined. If the double cup in the chain wheel is pitted, this should be pressed out and a new one fitted ; the cone and clutch-sleeve body also replaced if necessary. If these are in order a new set of balls can be fitted or one of the shim washers fitted between the clutch body and the cone removed to take up any play. The principal point to remember when adjusting

Fig. 3 .—DISMANTLING SINGLE-SPRING CLUTCH.

This shows how to unscrew the slotted locking ring by using a " Cee " spanner. But first screw two long screws into the two holes in the thrust plate, as described in the text.

this bearing is that the cone must be punched right home with the bearing still free. Any tendency to bind or run stiff must be overcome by fitting more shim washers. Do not forget to replace the locking washer.

Reassembling the Clutch

Clean the plates and the grooves in the clutch chain wheel, and reassemble in the reverse order to that already given. Insert the timing-cover screws to compress the springs, and refit the locking ring, which can be adjusted to the required spring pressure. Any tendency of " clutch slip " should be overcome by tightening this locking ring.

MEDIUM - WEIGHT TYPE CLUTCH

This is taken off the shaft by detaching the dome plate and unscrewing the hexagon sleeve nut in the centre of the clutch body. The clutch is then free to draw off the mainshaft. This clutch has one large spring, and is dismantled by undoing the locking ring. The clutch chain wheel rotates on 40 $\frac{3}{16}$-inch balls, held in position by two brass retainers. Take care these do not get mislaid when the chain wheel is lifted off.

B.S.A. GEARBOXES AND CLUTCHES

LIGHT - WEIGHT TYPE CLUTCH

This is a smaller edition of the medium type. The clutch is somewhat different, having eight small coil springs instead of the large single spring. The chain wheel idles on a series of balls in a brass retainer. The method of dismantling is similar to the other types, i.e. the clutch can be taken off complete. Difficulty is sometimes experienced in overcoming the spring pressure when trying to start the locking ring. A $\frac{5}{16}$-inch × 26T. bolt and nut with a large washer is supplied to facilitate this. The locking ring is held in position against the spring thrust plate, whilst the bolt is inserted through the washer and screwed into the threaded centre of the hexagon sleeve nut. The nut on the bolt is then screwed down, forcing the washer and locking ring into contact with the spring plate, and so overcoming the pressure of the springs until the clutch sleeve is met. The locking ring and the nut should now be turned together, when the former will pick up the thread on the sleeve, and can be screwed home until the desired pressure on the springs is reached. Heavy oil is recommended for B.S.A. gearboxes.

HEAVY - WEIGHT TYPE GEARBOX

THIS type is fitted to the big twin and some 5·57-h.p. models, and can be identified by the filler plug on the side-cover plate. The box is carried on the chain stays, clamped by two studs and a grooved plate. Before the nuts and the clamp plate are taken off the clutch should be removed. The gearbox can then be taken from the frame.

Dismantling the Gearbox

With the clutch off this is a simple matter. Draw off the kick-starter crank by driving out the cotter pin. Take off the end cover : a tap on the end of the mainshaft will loosen this after the screws have been taken out. The gears with operating shaft can then be withdrawn. The rear driving sprocket is still fitted to the top-gear pinion sleeve. This can be taken out if necessary by punching the locking washer clear and unscrewing the locking ring. The kick-starter quadrant and idler pinion are left in the box, and the latter can be taken out by undoing the left-handed pin on the clutch side of the gearbox.

Slipping out of Engagement

This is usually caused by worn operating forks and dog clutches, broken plunger spring or gear control out of adjustment. New operating forks are fitted by driving out the peg through the hole on the underside of the fork and fitting a new fork. It is advisable always to replace with a new peg. The gears are positioned by a spring-loaded plunger, which locates with a series of grooves cut in a quadrant fitted through the end cover. The quadrant is actuated by the control lever on the outside of the gearbox. If the plunger spring is broken the hexagon bush in which this slides should be unscrewed and the spring replaced.

B.S.A. GEARBOXES AND CLUTCHES

Oil Leakage

Provided the box is not overfilled with oil, leakage is usually due to worn retaining washers. These are thin steel disks fitted either side of the main-bearing ballrace. It is necessary to drive out the ballrace, fitting one washer between the race and the casing and the other between the top-gear pinion and the other side of the race when refitting the pinion.

Reassembling the Gearbox

After the top-gear pinion has been fitted, the kick-starter shaft should be fitted to the quadrant and the idler pinion replaced. The gears can be assembled with the operating shaft, forks, etc., and replaced into the box. The operating shaft should then be rotated so that the top gear is engaged. The quadrant on the end cover has four grooves cut in the circumference that engage with the plunger. Three of these are close together, and register first, neutral and second gears, whilst the fourth, which is farther removed, locates top gear. This one should be engaged with the plunger and the end cover refitted. The gears are now correctly timed. The gear lever on the tank should be placed in the top-gear position and the rod connected up. The latter can be lengthened or shortened by rotating the sleeve connecting the two halves of the rod. The two locking nuts must first be loosened. This adjustment must also be carried out when the gearbox is moved to adjust the chains.

MEDIUM - WEIGHT TYPE GEARBOX

In this type box the kick-starter quadrant is fitted to the layshaft directly inside the end cover. The order of dismantling is very similar to the heavy type. On 4·93-h.p. models this type of gearbox is fitted with heavy gears and clutch.

Engaging Gears

The method of operating the gears is the same as in the heavy box, and these are located by a spring plunger. The cause of second gear slipping out of engagement is often due to excessive endplay on the layshafts, owing to the shoulder of the bush in the kick-starter quadrant wearing away and allowing the pinion to slide from the dog clutch. This can be checked by pulling and pushing the lower end of the kick-starter crank towards and away from the gearbox. The remedy is to rebush the quadrant.

DESCRIPTION OF OPERATION

Four-Speed Gearbox. The four-speed gearbox is of the counter-shaft type, with all pinions in constant mesh and external clutch of the dry-plate type. Gear-changing is affected by sliding dog clutches *A* and *B*, and the method by which the dog-clutches are given the necessary movement constitutes one of the principal

41

features of the device (see Fig. 4). On shaft C, which is rotated by the pinion, and quadrant D (Fig. 5), which is operated by a lever at side of the tank, are mounted two operating forks E and F, the arms of which engage in the grooves of the dog clutches A and B. Helical cam grooves are formed in these forks, which engage pegs G fixed in shaft C. When shaft C is revolved by means of the operating mechanisms the pegs G cause the forks

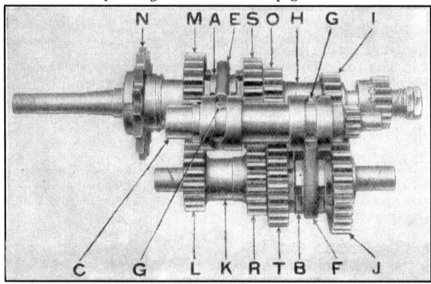

FIG. 4. INTERNAL VIEW OF THE FOUR-SPEED GEAR

E and F to slide along, the cams being cut so as to give the required position to the sliding dog clutches A and B. When first gear is put into operation dog clutch B is moved into engagement with pinion J. The drive is transmitted by means of central shaft pinion J. The drive is transmitted by means of central shaft H and pinion I to pinion J, then through dog clutch B to shaft K and pinion L, which in turn drives pinion M, to which the rear chain sprocket N is attached.

The second gear is obtained by rotating shaft C, which withdraws dog clutch B from engagement with pinion J into engagement with pinion T. The drive is then transmitted from shaft H through pinions L and T, then, as previously, through pinion L to pinion M (Fig. 10) and rear chain sprocket. Third gear is obtained in a similar manner through pinions R and S.

Fourth or high gear is effected by a further movement of shaft C, which withdraws dog clutch B from pinion T and engages dog clutch A with pinion M, clutch B being retained in an inoperative position.

Pinion sleeve *M*, with sprocket *N*, is thus coupled direct to shaft *H*, pinions *J*, *T*, *R* and *L* revolving idly. A means of ensuring correct position of all gears is arranged in the gearbox operating mechanism. The quadrant *D* (Fig. 5) is formed with teeth round part of its circumference only. On the plain portion of the periphery a number of pockets are provided, which engage with a spring plunger mounted on boss of gearbox cover The position of the gear lever in relation to the gear is thus assured if the control rod is correctly adjusted. To start the engine the operating lever is moved to the neutral position. Each dog clutch is now out of engagement. Movement of the kick-starter crank rotates quadrant *P* (Fig. 9) mounted on shaft *K*, which in turn engages with ratchet pinion mounted on shaft *H*. In order that its engagement shall be certain, without jamming, the first tooth in quadrant *P* is of special form. All difficulty of engagement is thus obviated. On the road the engine can only be started by means of the kick-starter with the gear in "neutral" position.

Three-speed Gear (2·49 h.p. S.V., and 2·49 h.p. O.H.V. Single Port). The drive on top gear is effected by sliding pinion *A* so that its dog teeth engage with those on pinion *B* (see Fig. 5). The middle gear is obtained by first withdrawing pinion *A* from engagement with pinion *B* and then sliding pinion *C* so that its dog teeth engage with fixed pinion *D*. Low gear is obtained by disengaging pinion *C* from pinion *D*, then sliding pinion *A* into

Fig. 5. Arrangement of the Gears on the Light Three-speed Gearbox

engagement with loose pinion *E*. The necessary axial movement of the gears *A* and *C* on their shafts is obtained by means of the operating forks *F* and *G* respectively, which engage in grooves in the gears.

Pegs on the control shaft *H* (see Fig. 6) working in helical cam slots in the forks convert the rotary movement of the outside gear lever (through a quadrant and gear) into the sliding motion of the operating forks. A spring-controlled plunger *J* on the gear control lever registering in depression in the control plate gives definite location to the gears.

FIG. 6. GEARBOX END-PLATE
ON THE LIGHT THREE-SPEED
GEARBOX

The Three-speed Countershaft Gear fitted to the 9·86 h.p. W.T. Model No. 13. This three-speed gearbox is of the countershaft type, with all pinions in constant mesh, and an external clutch of the dry-plate variety. (See Fig. 7).

The Dog Clutch. The changing of gears is effected by sliding dog clutches *A* and *B* (Fig. 10), and the method by which the dog clutches are given the necessary movement constitutes one of the principal features of the device. (See also Figs. 7, 8, and 9.)

On the shaft *C* (Fig. 10), which is rotated by means of the pinion and quadrant, which is operated by the lever at the side of the tank, are mounted two operating forks *E* and *F*, the arms of which engage in the grooves of the dog clutches *A* and *B*. Helical cam grooves are formed in these forks, which engage pegs *G* fixed in shaft *C*. When the shaft *C* is revolved by means of the operating mechanism, the pegs *G* cause the forks *E* and *F* to slide along, the cams being cut so as to give the required position to the sliding dog clutches, *A* and *B*.

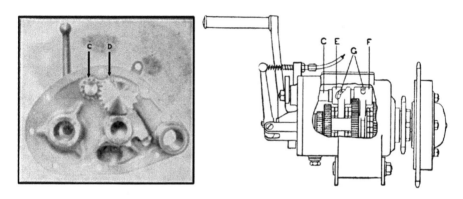

FIG. 7. THREE-SPEED GEARBOX END-PLATE As FITTED TO THE 9.86 H.P. W.T. MODEL

FIG. 8. THREE-SPEED GEARBOX (Outside View)

The Low Gear. When the low gear is put into operation, the dog clutch *B* is moved into engagement with pinion *J*. The drive is transmitted by means of central shaft *H* and pinion *I* to pinion *J*, then through dog clutch *B* to shaft *K* and pinion *L*, which in turn drives pinion *M*, to which the rear chain sprocket *N* is attached. (Fig. 10).

The Second Gear. The second gear is obtained by rotating shaft *C*, which withdraws dog clutch *B* from engagement with pinion *J* into engagement with pinion *T*. The drive is then transmitted from shaft *H* through pinions *O* and *T*, then, as previously, through pinion *L* to pinion *M* and rear chain sprocket. (Fig. 10).

The High Gear. The high or normal gear is effected by a further rotating of shaft *C*, which withdraws dog clutch *B* from pinion *T*, and engages dog clutch *A* with pinion *M*, clutch *B* being retained in an inoperative position. Pinion sleeve *M*, with sprocket *N*, is thus coupled direct to shaft *H*, pinions *J*, *T*, and *L* revolving idly. When changing up from low to high gear it is imperative that the drive of the engine should be disengaged momentarily by releasing the clutch. (Fig. 10).

B.S.A. GEARBOXES AND CLUTCHES

Engagement of Dog Clutches. A novel means of ensuring correct position of all gears is arranged in the gearbox operating mechanism. The quadrant D is formed with teeth round part of its circumference only. On the plain portion of the periphery a number of pockets are provided, which engage with a spring plunger mounted on the boss of the gearbox cover. The spring plunger on change lever is thus dispensed with. (Fig. 9).

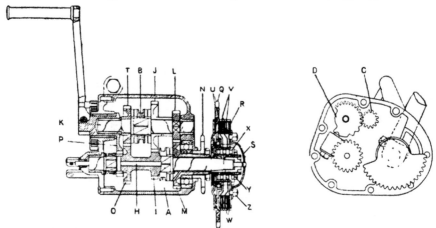

FIG. 9. THREE-SPEED GEARBOX (Inside View)

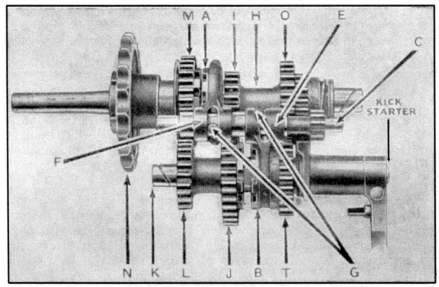

FIG. 10. AN INTERNAL VIEW OF THE GEAR-
BOX, WITH THE CLUTCH REMOVED

THE BURMAN GEARBOX

By R. O. Stirman

THE gearbox transmits the engine power to the road wheels, and is thus a very important factor in the modern motor-cycle. It is such an accepted feature nowadays that it is hard to realise that only a few years ago gearboxes were practically unheard of. Although they have contributed in no small way to the adaptability of the motor-cycle, and enabled designers to use such small-capacity engines, it is surprising how little the average rider knows about his gearbox.

The Burman gearbox may be divided into four sections, viz. gears, clutch, shock absorber and kick-starter, and we will therefore describe it in this order.

The Gears

The gears on all models (except the model " D," which has now been obsolete for some years) are always in mesh, and changes are made by means of dog clutches of ample dimensions. This minimises all risk of damaging the gears if a faulty change be made. The gear assembly can be seen at a glance from Fig. 1, and though this varies slightly in different models, the general arrangement is very much the same.

On the three-speed unit, gear positions in top, middle and bottom are locked when in place by a patent rack and pawl mechanism inside the box. This allows a clean silent change to be made without fear of missing or running through the gear desired. All the parts of this mechanism are immersed in lubricant, and are actuated by a bell-crank lever which is in turn operated by a lever connected directly to the control.

The four-speed gearbox is of the type using four sets of gears, and is so designed that each of the two pairs of gears are mounted close to the ends of the shaft, thus resulting in exceptional silence. The sliding members are controlled by operating forks working on a cam, the movements being geared up to the actuating lever. In order to minimise any friction, the cam itself is mounted on roller bearings, this giving an exceptionally easy change, while the gear positions are positively located inside the gearbox.

The Clutch

This, in all models (excepting the new lightweight model " G," which has a single plate clutch), is of the multi-plate type, running dry, and consists of a number of cork-inserted plates running in conjunction with plain steel plates, and operated by a rod passing through the centre of the

47

mainshaft. The one end of the rod is held in a recessed adjusting screw in the clutch spring plate, while the other bears against a hardened steel ball in the operating lever.

Fabric or Cork for Clutches ?

There has been a good deal of controversy on the subject of cork versus asbestos fabric as a friction material for clutches. Our recommendation is as follows : for ordinary touring, traffic work, road racing and sprint racing, cork is by far the best material ; but for sand racing, motor-cycle football, and freak trials, we recommend fabric. Briefly, the advantages and disadvantages of each are these : cork possesses greater gripping power, is unaffected by oil or water, and being slightly elastic takes up the drive of the engine in a smooth, progressive and shockless manner. Cork, however, will not stand continued slipping, as it is liable to char and burn.

Fabric, on the other hand, does not grip so well as cork, and therefore needs a stronger spring pressure to carry the same load ; it is liable to slip when exposed to oil or water, and is very fierce on taking up the load, due to its hardness and incompressibility. It will, however, not burn out when slipped continuously, although under such conditions it quickly becomes glazed, and will not transmit the same load as before unless provided with a new surface.

It should be noted that when in use the cork expands slightly, and to allow for this expansion a gap of at least $\frac{1}{32}$ inch must be left between the end of the clutch-operating rod and the ball in the clutch lever. Failure to do this will result in the clutch failing to operate.

If there is Sideplay in Chainwheel

All models previous to January 1927 have a ballrace in the clutch chainwheel. This consists of two hardened steel cones separated by thin pen-steel washers. If wear occurs in this ballrace (noticeable byplay from side to side in the chainwheel), the race should be taken apart, one or more of the spacing washers withdrawn and the race reassembled. The chainwheel should run perfectly freely, but without sideways movement. In models after January 1927 a roller race (see Fig. 2) is fitted, this being stronger and more durable than the old type, and needs no adjustment whatsoever.

Shock Absorber

In all Burman boxes a shock absorber is fitted to the clutch chainwheel in such a way that the drive is transmitted from the chainwheel to the clutch through rubber buffers. These, while being perfectly rigid laterally, allow a radial movement of approximately $\frac{3}{16}$ inch, which is amply sufficient to absorb any ordinary harshness (see Fig. 2).

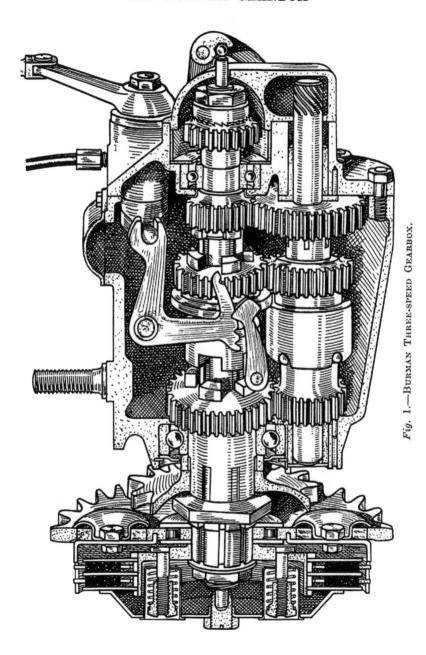

Fig. 1.—BURMAN THREE-SPEED GEARBOX.

Fig. 2.—Clutch Parts laid out in Order of Removal.

The roller race is shown, also the shock absorbers in the clutch chainwheel. Many people think the hexagon head shown in the centre of the gearbox casing is a level screw for checking the oil level. This, however, is the stud that secures the pawl which locates the gear position. This stud is split pinned, and if an attempt is made to remove the stud inadvertently, the end will be broken off, necessitating dismantling of the gearbox.

The Kick-starter

This is entirely separate from the major portion of the box, and is only in operation during the actual process of starting, the pedal-driven quadrant rotating the mainshaft through a ratchet wheel; thus, the transmission gears are not used for kick-starting purposes.

The speedometer drive is obtained through a pair of spirals, one of which is mounted on the layshaft.

Taking the Gearbox to Pieces

As a gearbox is a difficult piece of work to handle without special tackle, it will be found more convenient to start the process of dissembling when the gearbox is still in the frame.

Three-speed Models

In cases where a band is fitted on the clutch this should be removed, the clutch-adjusting nuts unscrewed, and the clutch springs, spring cups and spring plate should be taken off. The clutch plates may then be removed, and should be preserved in the same order so they may be replaced in the same relative positions. This will expose the nut holding the clutch on the mainshaft, which should be unscrewed (first putting into gear and applying rear brake so as to lock the gearbox), and the clutch may be removed bodily.

In the case of models " R," " W " and " T," the clutch is castellated on to the mainshaft, and can readily be taken apart, exposing the roller race and the clutch shock absorbers. In the case of all other models, the clutch body holds the chainwheel on its race, and should be removed by giving a sharp tap on the end of the mainshaft with a piece of soft metal, while pressure is exerted between the clutch and the driving sprocket. This should loosen the clutch assembly on the taper, which can then be removed in its entirety.   The domed bracket holding the clutch lever should then be removed from the opposite end of the box by undoing the two screws provided.   This will expose the kick-starter ratchet mechanism, which, in the case of the models " E," " L," " R," " W " and " T," is secured by a single nut which can be unscrewed.   In the case of models " M," " O " and " Q," there are two nuts, the second of which, the driving ratchet, must be removed with a tubular spanner.   The cover plate over the kick-starter quadrant should be removed, and the kick-starter with its quadrant and spring can then be removed from its axle.

The gearbox can now, if desired, be removed from the frame and the remaining parts dissembled.   The nuts holding the endplate should be removed, and the whole endplate will then be free to slide from the gearbox.   The mainshaft can then be removed.   In the case of models " R," " W " and " T," it should slide out from the clutch end, as the castellated diameter on which the clutch is mounted will not slide through the driving gear.   In all other models the mainshaft should slide towards the kick-starter end of the gearbox.

Removing Assembly from Gearbox

The screw at the bottom of the box controlling the pawl spring can be removed, together with the spring.   It will now be found that the complete gear assembly can be removed from the gearbox, with the exception of the driving gear, with its ball bearings and rear sprocket attached.   There is no necessity for these parts to be removed unless the rear sprocket and driving gear show any sideways movement, which points to the ballrace being worn.   The layshaft bearings can easily be inspected, and if they show signs of play should be renewed if necessary.

Reassembling

It is important when reassembling that the two sliding gears should be properly meshed one with the other by means of the flanges provided for the purpose, and also that the operating lever block on the bellcrank lever should be in position on the mainshaft sliding gear.

On no account should force be used if difficulty in reassembling is found, as all the parts should slide into position without any force being necessary, otherwise damage will result.

If the gears and inside of the box have been cleaned with paraffin after dissembling, the various bearings should be oiled before reassembly.

It should be noted that there are no left-hand threads in the manufacture of the gearbox with the exception of the kick-starter lever in the models where this is screwed to the kick-starter quadrant.   Except in cases where the quadrant needs renewing, these two parts should not be dissembled.

Avoiding Trouble in assembling Kick-starter

Sometimes trouble is occasioned when reassembling the kick-starter mechanism and spring. If a new spring is to be fitted this should be assembled with the spring tightly coiled and bound with wire. This presents no trouble whatever, and when assembled the wire should be cut with a pair of pliers and removed. If, however, it is desired to refit an old spring, the following procedure should be adopted. Attach each end of the spring to its correct pin and slide the kick-starter on to its centre pin. Keeping the kick-starter at the top of the centre pin, wind the spring up two to two and a half turns, keeping the coils from riding over each other by means of a screwdriver, then gradually work the kick-starter down to its correct position, using the screwdriver with the other hand to keep the spring in position. The description may sound difficult, but actually in practice it will be found to slip into place quite easily (see Figs. 3 and 4).

Four-speed Models

To dismantle the gears the outer operating lever should first be removed and the small nuts holding the aluminium end cover unscrewed; the end will then come away without difficulty, and it should be noticed that it is not necessary to remove the kick-starter operating lever (Fig. 5).

The gear quadrant and cam spindle can be taken away, and the mainshaft nut holding the kick-starter mechanism can be unscrewed, and it will then be possible, by unscrewing the nuts holding the kick-starter case, to remove this latter part, thus exposing the interior of the gearbox. Care should be taken not to lose the rollers forming the roller race on the cam spindle. Next unscrew the pawl spring plug at the bottom of the gearbox to allow the removal of the spring, after which the entire gear assembly, together with cam spindle and operating forks, can be removed from the gearbox.

To reassemble Four-speed Models

To reassemble, the reverse procedure should be followed, first assembling the operating forks on to their respective gears and sliding dog, and then sliding these into position in the gearbox. If the mainshaft is first replaced this will assist in locating the gears in their correct position. The rollers for the cam spindle should be held in place on their groove by smearing with thick grease and the kick-starter case can then be assembled.

It is important to assemble the gear control quadrant to the corresponding gear on the cam spindle, so that the marked teeth in each

THE BURMAN GEARBOX

item coincide. The cam spindle may be more easily turned if the pawl spring is not refitted until after this operation has been completed. The clutch-operating lever lug on the outer cover prevents the kick-starter crank being turned the complete circumference, and so it is necessary to rewind the kick-

Fig. 4 (Below).— SPRING WOUND UP AND THE STOP BEING FITTED.

*Fig. 3.—*REFITTING A KICK-STARTER SPRING—FIRST POSITION.

starter spring and bind with wire, this being cut after the case is located on its fixing studs, but before pushing into place, the kick-starter being pulled down slightly in order that the quadrant may clear the kick-starter stop.

Foot Control

This popular fitting is designed so that there is little likelihood of

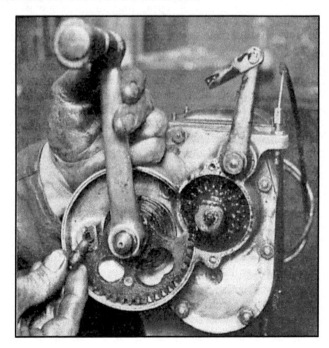

any trouble being experienced by the rider. Briefly its operation is as follows :

A double-edged pawl which is pivoted engages with the ratchet teeth cut on the convex surface of a sector which is keyed to the spindle carrying the control inner lever. Behind the pawl and ratchet is the body casting, which is also pivoted on the spindle. On the back of this casing are two bosses, which bear against stops on the bush, and thus limit the movement of the lever. For this reason it is impossible to miss a gear, and springs in the body return the lever to the same position after each change has been made.

To dismantle the Foot Control

With three-speed models it is advisable to remove the kick-starter case complete with the control, for whilst by the removal of the two hexagon nuts which secure the lever the entire control may be dismantled, on reassembling it will probably be found that the control inner lever has come out of the slots on the sleeve. When refitting, care should be taken to see that the trunnion ball on the inner lever is fitting properly in the bell crank.

Reassembly of Foot Control

The earlier four-speed models are fitted with a double diameter sleeve, and riders having this type may experience a little difficulty in reassembling.

First rebuild the complete foot control on to the kick-starter cover together with the sector, then mark with chalk the edges of the two teeth between which the tooth marked with an " O " on the cam spindle has to mesh, then slide the kick-starter cover over the fixing pins, making sure that the sector teeth mesh correctly.

On the later models the sleeve is a single diameter, allowing the sector to be assembled first, after which the cover can be fitted and the foot control built up last. It should be noted that the ratchet is marked to ensure it being refitted correctly.

Lubrication with Grease

Every box leaves the works charged with grease, and is safe to run without attention for at least 1,000 miles. It sometimes happens that a box is slightly overcharged with grease to ensure a supply reaching every part of the bearings, and this surplus may work its way out of the box. It will, however, cease after a few miles, and the grease having found its normal level, no further escape will occur.

Not Oil

We do not recommend the use of oil in Burman gearboxes. After exhaustive tests we find that a light type of grease, such as Wakefield's

Castrolease Medium, or if this is not procurable, Gargoyle Mobilubricant Extra Soft, is the most satisfactory in every way. This effectually lubricates the wearing parts while not being subject to changes in viscosity to the same extent as gear oil, and it actually results in less loss through friction and churning than does oil.

As regards replenishment, this should be carried out every 1,000 to 1,500 miles, about 3 to 4 oz. of grease being required. It is important not to fill the box, as this will result in the throwing out of the grease when the gears are revolving at high speed (exerting a considerable pumping action). To obtain best results, the box should be about one-third full.

Fig. 5.—END COVER OF THE FOUR-SPEED BOX REMOVED.

The kick-starter quadrant, crank and spring come away with the cover. The speedometer driving worm is seen at the bottom of the box, whilst the gear-operating rack will be noted on the cover and the pinion on the gearbox.

Don't use Heavy Grease

On no account should heavy grease be used to lubricate the gearbox, as this tends, besides causing difficulty in operation, to be thrown to the sides of the gearbox, leaving the gears to run without adequate lubricant. If in cases of emergency no suitable grease is obtainable, a thicker grease can be used, provided a sufficient quantity of ordinary engine oil is mixed with it to reduce its consistency. The gearbox should always be refilled with the correct lubricant as soon as possible. For long-distance races and fast touring we recommend light grease with the addition of about 25 per cent. of engine oil. For sprint races the gearbox should be washed out, and a minimum quantity of thin oil can be used.

Apart from the gears, the clutch cable wire should be removed occasionally and greased, also the clutch operating rod. The clutch roller race should be packed with grease every 5,000 to 7,000 miles, and the clutch operating lever and other joints should be oiled fairly frequently.

Gear Ratios

The rider can determine the gear ratios of the machine he is using in the following manner :

$$\text{Top gear} = \frac{\text{Number of teeth in back hub sprocket} \times \text{Number of teeth in clutch sprocket.}}{\text{Number of teeth in engine sprocket} \times \text{Number of teeth in driving sprocket.}}$$

This gives the top gear ratio, and other ratios can be obtained by multiplying this figure by the ratios given in our leaflets relating to the various types of gearboxes. For example, if the top gear is determined as being 5 to 1, and the ratios in the gearbox are given in our leaflet as 1–1·62–2·64, the complete ratios will be 5–8·10–13·20.

GEARBOX TROUBLES—THEIR CAUSE AND CURE

The following is a brief summary of the various troubles occasionally experienced by the rider.

Clutch Slip

This may be due to several causes :

(a) Clutch not engaging properly, due to mal-adjustment. See that Bowden cable is free in its casing (it may have stuck, and thus be holding the clutch out) and that the clutch lever works freely. Also make sure that the requisite $\frac{1}{32}$ inch clearance is allowed between the clutch rod and ball in clutch lever.

(b) In the case of fabric clutches, slip may be caused by oil or water on the clutch plates. Remove plates, clean thoroughly and replace.

(c) Insufficient spring tension. The clutch springs are adjustable for tension and can be tightened up with a screwdriver. They should not be screwed up solid or clutch will not withdraw ; the correct adjustment is when the spring nuts are just flush with the endplate.

Clutch not Freeing

This is either due to wear on the clutch rod, which can be allowed for by adjustment of the screw and lock nut in centre of spring plate ; or to overtightening of the clutch springs. It may also be due to too much slack in the Bowden cable, caused by stretching of the wire. This slack can be taken up by unscrewing the cable adjuster or by means of the adjustment provided on the spring plate on clutch (as described above).

It may also be caused by the tongues on the clutch plates wearing grooves in the clutch case. This is caused by wear on the chainwheel race, which allows the clutch case to oscillate relative to the clutch plates, causing excessive wear. The clutch race should be adjusted or renewed, if necessary, and if the clutch plates and clutch case are so badly worn as to require renewing also, this should be done.

Gears Jumping Out

This is nearly always due to the non-coincidence of gear positions in the box with that of the gear lever in the gate. This results from movement of the gearbox for purposes of chain adjustment and subsequent failure to check over the gear positions. This is quickly put right by adjustment of length of control rod.

It is sometimes due to weakening of the pawl spring, which controls the gear selector mechanism inside the box.

Gears Hard to Operate

This may be due to stiffness in the control joints, too strong a pawl spring or too thick a grease in the gearbox, this latter being a frequent source of trouble.

Gears " Crashing " when changing Up or Down

Frequently this is due to mal-adjustment of gears. It is not necessary with Burman gears to double declutch either up or down, and if a very quick or " racing " change is desired, very little pressure should be put on the clutch. It should not be fully withdrawn, but merely eased, when a perfect change will result.

Clutch Sprocket Loose

If the clutch chainwheel can be moved relative to the clutch case, it is a sign that the shock absorber rubbers are wearing, and should be replaced.

If, however, there is no movement between the chainwheel and the clutch case, but the two together can be rocked from side to side, then the ball or roller race inside the chainwheel needs adjustment. In the case of the ballrace, this play can be taken up by removing the clutch, taking apart the races and removing one or more of the small spacing washers. With the roller race about $\frac{1}{64}$ inch endplay is permissible : if more is found, then wear has taken place, and probably new rollers are required.

Clutch Springs becoming Unscrewed

When a clutch is operated, the springs each tend to rotate slightly. Normally this is quite insufficient to unscrew the holding-down nut, but if, as sometimes happens, the springs are fastened by rust, mud or similar conditions to the nut, the nuts may become unscrewed. The remedy is to clean the springs and nuts, polish the ends of the springs by rubbing on emery cloth, and reassemble with a touch of grease or oil on the nuts and springs.

OVERHAUL AND ADJUSTMENT OF THE DOUGLAS GEARBOX AND FLYWHEEL CLUTCH

By S. GILL

FLYWHEEL CLUTCH

This type of clutch has been fitted as standard on Douglas machines for a number of years, and whilst over this period they have varied in construction in a number of different ways, there are actually only two distinct types, all the others being modifications of these.

The construction of the A/31 clutch, which is the same as that fitted to all engines marked Y.E., E.H., E.N. and E.V., is as follows: the flywheel, which also acts as a clutch body, the back plate, the centre plate, to which is attached the friction linings, and the pressure plate upon which the springs act. In addition there are of course the parts for the clutch operation. With this type it will be noticed that the driving power is transmitted by means of gripping the driven plate between the pressure plate and the back plate.

Dealing with Clutch Slip

To alter the load capacity of the clutch the nut outside of the driven plate needs to be adjusted to give the required grip. If excessive pressure needs to be put upon the springs to overcome slip, it shows that either the linings are dirty, badly worn, or the plates distorted. After an examination it is only necessary to true or renew any damaged parts.

Dealing with Clutch Drag

The same steps have to be taken to overcome excessive clutch drag. The pressure plate is driven by means of pegs which pass through the face of the flywheel, and after a certain amount of running a clutch rattle may set up. The best method of overcoming this is to drill new holes of the correct diameter in a different position in the flywheel, and fill in the original holes.

Stiff or Noisy Clutch

Stiff or noisy clutch operation is usually brought about owing to worn faces on operating cam and clutch body, and whilst it is possible to grind these faces and make them perfectly true, it will usually be found that the hardening is damaged, and only by the fitting of new parts would the repair become a lasting one. Clutch sticking out is usually brought about owing to uneven wear of the pins on which the operating cam works, or because some of the operating parts are being held out when used.

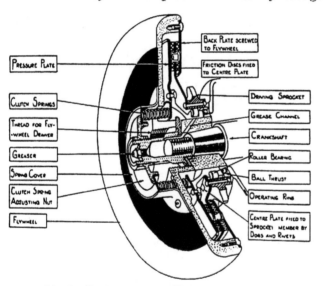

Fig. 1.—SECTION OF THE FLYWHEEL CLUTCH.

This shows the construction of the A/31 clutch. Note how the centre clutch plate is gripped between the spring-operated pressure plate and the back plate of the flywheel, thus transmitting the driving power.

Special Note on Clutch Adjustment

It is important to remember that as the adjusting nut is screwed up to accommodate wear of the friction material, the operating arm must be likewise adjusted by lengthening the Bowden wire, otherwise the spring pressure is exerted on the thrust race instead of the pressure plate.

Clutch Assembly

In assembling after overhaul, the whole of the parts, with the exception of the springs, flywheel nut and adjusting nut, can be assembled and placed on the crankshaft as a single unit. Whilst provision is made for the use of six springs, a less number should be used wherever possible, and with the light models, three springs should be found to be sufficient at all times.

A/31 CLUTCH · DISMANTLING AND ADJUSTING

After a considerable amount of mileage has been covered, the constant use of the clutch in changing gear, slipping in traffic and in getting away from a standstill, a certain amount of wear is inevitable, and so a suitable means of adjustment is provided. When taking up the wear on the friction linings on the adjusting screw, lengthen the Bowden cable by means of the adjuster, provided otherwise the spring pressure will be exerted on the ball bearing and in turn on the cam face instead of the pressure plate. It is essential that there should be $\frac{1}{16}$ in. play between the operating cam and the release thrust race, and to make certain of this allow some free movement on the clutch lever control before hand pressure enables the clutch to be withdrawn. The first item to be tackled when the clutch is being dismantled is the flywheel lock-nut which should be undone and the driving key removed. The spring pressure adjusting nut, together with the springs and ring, may be removed next. The flywheel withdrawal tool should then be screwed into the flywheel boss until it touches the end of the crankshaft. Hammer the tool round an extra turn and then strike it sharply, when the flywheel should be jarred off the taper on the crankshaft. Some of the Douglas models are fitted with self-extracting flywheels in which case it is only necessary to unscrew the flywheel nut. When the clutch is dismantled, it should be carefully cleaned out as particles of dust tend to disintegrate from the friction linings. Should this be allowed to clog up between the periphery of the clutch plate and flywheel it will eventually result in the clutch refusing to function. If upon examination, the Raybestos lining appears in good condition the clutch may be replaced, but if any slipping has been experienced and the friction lining shows signs of considerable wear, the plate should be returned to the makers to be relined. Absolute accuracy is essential when fitting new friction linings as any mis-alinement will create a tendency to vibration caused through part of the rotating mass being out of balance. In reassembling, the clutch unit, with the exception of the springs, flywheel nut and washer, or driving key and adjusting nut, may be placed on the crankshaft as a complete unit. There should be at least $\frac{1}{16}$ in. clearance between the end of the shaft and the face of the flywheel boss, with the flywheel forced on the shaft. With this correct, screw up the lock-nut. Make absolutely certain that the lock-nut is securely tightened, otherwise there is a danger of the flywheel working loose. With the lock-nut in place the four springs should be inserted, and their retaining washer put into place.

D/31 CLUTCH · DISMANTLING AND ADJUSTING

The clutch as fitted to Model D/31, and all models of similar construction, is quite different, although in general the earlier remarks apply as regards adjustments and repair. The driven plate has one lining only, and this acts direct on to the back plate by means of pressure, which is exerted through the bearing ring. The friction material used with this clutch is either raybestos or cork inserts. It is essential that the plates of this clutch be kept true, as only two faces are in contact, and if excessive

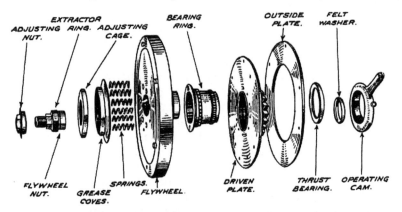

Fig. 2.—CLUTCH PARTS OF MODELS E.Q. AND E.R.
The driven plate acts on the outside plate through pressure by the bearing ring.

drag or slip is noticed the back plate should be removed and tested for truth. Should this plate be distorted to any extent, a new one should be obtained, as the truing of this plate usually proves to be ineffective owing to the fact that immediately it gets warm it will again distort to its old shape. Should the faces on which the operating thrust race bears become worn, they should be ground and new thrust rings fitted. These rings are a standard fitment on the latest models.

In the event of clutch slip being experienced it is possible to increase the spring pressure by turning the adjusting nut (plated and situated in the centre of the flywheel) *clockwise*. The Bowden cable should then be adjusted by means of the milled disk to correspond to the new spring pressure. Remember when effecting this adjustment that the operating cam should lift to a distance of approximately $\frac{3}{16}$ in. before commencing to lift the clutch.

To dismantle the clutch, first remove the front chain guard and then proceed to remove the adjusting nut, springs, cage, and grease cover. The flywheel is of the self-extracting type and may be taken off in the following manner: Apply a spanner to the flywheel nut which protrudes from the centre of the flywheel and hammer this round in an *anti-clockwise*

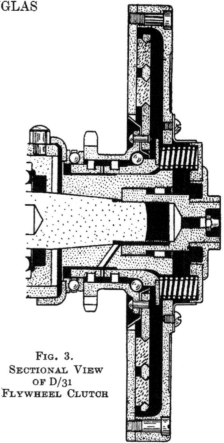

Fig. 3.
Sectional View
of D/31
Flywheel Clutch

direction. It will be found after moving a few threads that the nut is again tightening up, and at this point it is in contact with the extractor ring. By exerting further force on the nut with the spanner and hammer the flywheel will be gradually withdrawn.

Having removed the flywheel the clutch can be lifted out after first removing the back plate, which is held by six screws. If an inspection reveals that the cork inserts are much worn, the best plan is to return the friction plate to the manufacturers, in order to have new corks fitted and properly faced. When reassembling the clutch it is very important to see that the clutch bearing ring or body slides freely on the flywheel boss, otherwise nice action will be impeded. Apply some Castrolease Medium to all bearings and the clutch bearing ring. In the ordinary way attention is seldom required, but whenever there is a tendency for clutch slip or "drag" it is advisable to overhaul the clutch as described above.

DOUGLAS GEARBOX AS FITTED TO ALL SIDE-VALVE MACHINES
FROM 1926 ONWARDS

The gears are of the simplest construction. The mainshaft carries a sliding pinion with a dog on either side. The sleeve pinion runs on the driving end of the shaft, and the low-gear pinion on the opposite end. The gear location is by means of a $\frac{3}{16}$-inch ball, which fits into

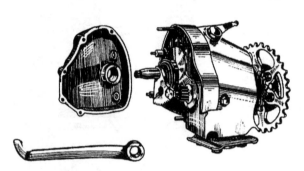

a spring-loaded hole inside the sliding pinion and engages into countersinks on the mainshaft. The layshaft has a pinion fixed at each end and four dogs in the middle of the shaft, on which the second gear operates. The pinions are pressed on to the shaft, and are located by means of two keys.

Fig. 4.—GEARBOX WITH COVER REMOVED.

Showing position of the spring and kick-starter quadrant.

Dismantling

To dismantle, remove chain wheel and driving sprocket. Take off kick-starter pedal, cover, quadrant, and then the end plate, which does not necessitate taking off the ratchet pinion or nut. Both shafts can then be lifted out of the box complete with gears (see Fig. 4).

Reassembling

To assemble the box, fit up mainshaft, complete with sleeve pinion, and layshaft complete, and assemble both together with the selector fork. Build up the drive-side roller bearing, when the whole of the gears can be placed into the box, care being necessary to get the slipper of the operating lever into its position on the operating fork.

How to adjust the Gearbox

To set the adjustment of gears proceed as follows : move the gear-change lever until the gears in the box are in neutral. Without moving the position of the gear rods or gears in the box, the gear-change lever must then be brought to register correctly in the neutral position in the gear gate on the tank. This is done by screwing up or unscrewing the nuts on each side of the swivel on the lower end of the lever. Should, for any reason, excessive wear take place, and it is found difficult to obtain all three gear positions correctly, it will be found that there is a second position provided on the bell-crank lever, and it is only necessary to fix the gear rod into the alternative position, when the trouble will be readily overcome.

DOUGLAS

The Douglas Three-Speed Gearbox. This is a countershaft box of normal design but, of course, minus the usual clutch mechanism. Fig. 2 shows the method of working. It will be observed that in the case of the Douglas gearbox the countershaft, or layshaft as it is more usually called, is placed *above* and not below the mainshaft. These two shafts are shown at L and M respectively. The layshaft has three pinions, namely D, N, and C, all of which, except N are rigidly attached to the shaft. Pinion N is free to slide and rotate on the layshaft, but can be locked to the shaft, which is splined at the centre only.

On the mainshaft there are four pinions K, B, S, and H, K is provided solely for the purpose of the kick-starter, and grips the mainshaft when rotated in an anti-clockwise direction. B is the low-gear dog wheel, and is free to rotate on the mainshaft, although always in constant mesh with the layshaft pinion D. Adjacent to the low-gear dog wheel B, and sliding on the splined portion of the mainshaft, is the sliding pinion S controlled by the selector mechanism P. To the right of this sliding pinion,

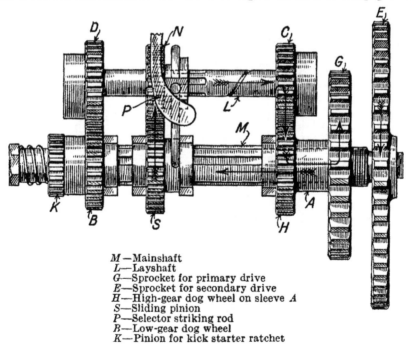

M—Mainshaft
L—Layshaft
G—Sprocket for primary drive
E—Sprocket for secondary drive
H—High-gear dog wheel on sleeve A
S—Sliding pinion
P—Selector striking rod
B—Low-gear dog wheel
K—Pinion for kick starter ratchet

FIG. 5.—DIAGRAM OF THE DOUGLAS THREE-SPEED GEARBOX OPERATION

which has dogs on either side and is always in mesh with the layshaft pinion *N*, which slides simultaneously with the mainshaft pinion *S*, is the high-gear dog wheel *H* in constant mesh with the layshaft pinion *C* and rigidly fixed to sleeve *A*, which can revolve independently of the mainshaft. Also attached to this sleeve is the sprocket *G* transmitting the secondary drive to the rear wheel. It will thus be seen that whenever the rear wheel is in motion, the layshaft also is in motion. The speed of the layshaft does, in fact, determine the speed of the rear wheel, and alterations in this speed are effected by means of the sliding pinions, *S* and *N*. Let us see how this is done, taking first the case illustrated by Fig. 5. *E* is the gearbox sprocket which receives the primary drive direct from the engine flywheel clutch sprocket and transmits it to the mainshaft. Now pinions *S* and *N* being in engagement, and pinion *N* locked to the layshaft, the drive is transmitted to the layshaft and back through the high-gear dog wheel to the rear wheel drive sprocket *G*. Pinion *B* rotates idly. The gear reduction that occurs is almost due completely

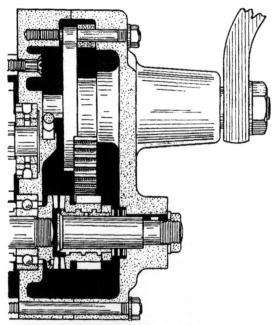

FIG. 6.—SHOWING THE LATEST CONSTANT-MESH KICK-STARTER

This totally enclosed design facilitates starting because it prevents jamming. It also reduces the risk of tooth breakage on the pinion or quadrant

to the difference in size between pinions C and H, and is roughly proportional to the difference between their diameters. Pinion S is slightly larger than pinion N, and therefore a slight increase in layshaft speed occurs, but a very considerable reduction takes place at the gearbox sprocket G due to the difference in size between pinions C and H. This is middle or second gear.

When sliding pinions are moved right over to the left so that the layshaft dogs engage with those of the low-gear dog wheel, we have two distinct gear reductions, that which takes place between pinions B and D and that due to pinions C and H. From the size of the pinions in the illustration it is at once clear that the resultant gear ratio, i.e. bottom gear is approximately twice as low as middle gear. The specifications show that this is so.

Neutral gear (i.e. clutch in, machine stationary with the engine running) is obtained by moving the sliding pinions half-way over to the left until the layshaft pinion is clear of the splines and the mainshaft pinion dogs not in contact with the low-gear dog wheel. In this case the mainshaft alone revolves, and when the clutch is lifted both shafts become stationary. It is thus impossible to cause damage when going from neutral into first or bottom gear so long as the engine is de-clutched, and the rear wheel is slightly moved to allow the dogs to engage.

Top gear is attained simply. The sliding pinions are carried right across to the right-hand until the dogs on the lower pinion mesh with those of the high-gear dog wheel H. The sleeve A then becomes locked to the mainshaft, and the two chain sprockets rotate at the same speed. The layshaft, of course, runs idle.

The gearbox selector plunger, consisting of a spring and ball in the middle gear pinion, automatically holds the gear in full engagement as the ball is forced by the spring into countersunk holes in the mainshaft.

Self-alining roller bearings are fitted to the mainshaft and ball-bearings of standard pattern to the layshaft.

The 1937–9 Douglas 600 c.c. model has a heavyweight four-speed gearbox of Douglas design and manufacture.

Gearbox. As the Douglas gearbox (Fig. 7) is a fixture in the frame and the operating lever works on the frame lug, adjustments are reduced to a minimum, apart from the very infrequent adjustment of the selector gear.

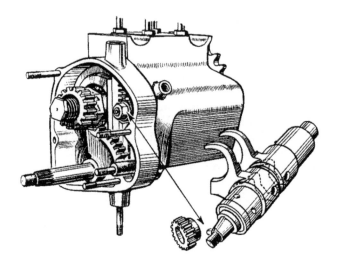

(*From "The Motor Cycle"*)

FIG. 7.—THE DOUGLAS FOUR-SPEED GEARBOX, SHOWING
RACK OPERATION

This type of gearbox has been used since 1934, but various modifications
were made during the following years, including an improved
constant mesh kick-starter mechanism as shown in Fig 6.

GEARBOX SHOCK ABSORBER · 1926 ONWARDS

On all models this is incorporated in the gearbox chainwheel, and is
made up as follows :

The Shock-absorber Body

This is fixed to the mainshaft of the gearbox by means of a taper
and two keys.

The Chainwheel

This is made up with six hardened thimbles to take plungers and
springs, which operate on—

The Cam Plate

The sliding action of these parts forms the effective part of the shock
absorber itself. The adjustment should be made so as to allow movement of the plungers on the face of the cam without it being possible for the
chainwheel to turn independently.

OVERHAUL AND ADJUSTMENT OF THE NEW HUDSON GEARBOX AND CLUTCH

By B. Bourke

The New Hudson gearbox was manufactured in two types. In 1927 the gearbox was suspended from the gearbox platform, whilst the 1928–30 pattern box was carried on top of the platform.

Externally, these gearboxes appear quite different, whilst internally the design is similar, though with the 1928–30 pattern the shafts and pinions are heavier, whilst the dogs of the pinions are practically twice as deep as the earlier 1927 type.

Assembling and dismantling is, to all intents and purposes, identical with both boxes; consequently, they can be treated collectively.

Assuming the gearbox has been removed from the frame, it should be thoroughly externally cleaned to facilitate clean handling. In the case

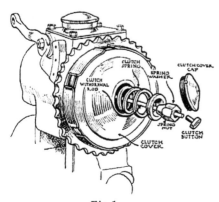

Fig. 1.
How to dismantle the clutch.

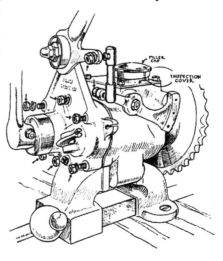

Fig. 2.—GEARBOX.
How the end cover is removed.

of the 1927 box, place the holding-down studs into the vice between lead clamps, with the clutch assembly towards the operator. However, with the 1930 box the thickened base of the gearbox, through which the fixing studs fit, should be placed in the vice.

Dismantling Clutch

Proceed to dismantle the clutch in the following manner :

Remove the small locking screw from the clutch-thrust cover plate, which will then permit the thrust cap to be unscrewed. To do this place the end of a brass drift into one of the notches round the cap, when one or two sharp blows with the hammer, applied to the drift, will cause the thrust cap to become loose, and it can then be removed by the fingers. This will lay bare the clutch-spring nut and withdrawal-rod endpin (or clutch button as it is sometimes called).

Order of Clutch Plates

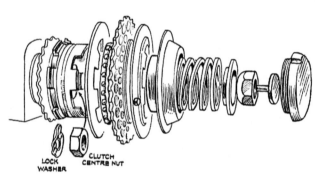

LOCK WASHER   CLUTCH CENTRE NUT

Fig. 3.—CLUTCH.
This shows the single-plate clutch dismantled.

The clutch-spring nut is screwed to the shaft by a right-hand thread. To remove the nut hold the clutch sprocket, and unscrew the nut, when the clutch spring, together with the clutch plates, can be withdrawn. The clutch is made up in the following manner : clutch-thrust cover cap, clutch-thrust plate, clutch outer plate, friction disk, friction plate, friction disk, centre plate, friction disk, clutch-chain ring, further friction disk, and the clutch back plate.

With the clutch plates removed, the clutch centre and rear-drive sprocket can be taken away. Knock back the clutch lock washer, place a fairly long screwdriver between the dogs of the clutch centre, holding the end of the screwdriver to prevent the clutch centre moving whilst the nut is being unscrewed.

With the nut taken away, place a small chisel between the sprocket lock nut and the back of the clutch centre in such a manner that it will not damage the shaft, when a sharp blow with a hammer applied to the head of the chisel will have the necessary effect of loosening the clutch centre on the shaft, leaving the key in position. Remove the key to a place of safety.

Removing Internals

Take the box from the vice, turn it round, replace it in the vice, and proceed to take out the gears. To do this, remove the six cover stud nuts, when the gearbox end cover, together with the clutch actuating arm and kick-starter crank, will come away.

The kick-starter ratchet pinion and the low pinion mainshaft are next taken out. Remove the gear-control quadrant, and unscrew from the box the control-fork bushes, when the control fork, together with the internal gears, with the exception of the mainshaft high pinion, can be taken out.

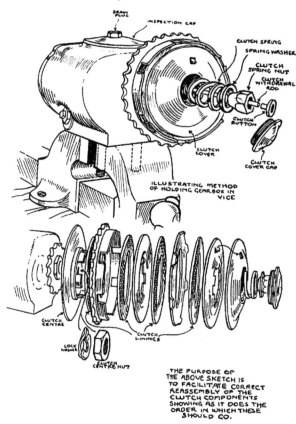

How to remove High-gear Pinion

To remove the high pinion take a piece of mild steel plate, about $\frac{1}{4}$ inch thick, 8 inches long, $1\frac{1}{2}$ inches wide. Place this vertically into the vice, then over this lower the gearbox housing until the high-pinion dogs engage with the piece of metal in the vice. The piece of plate will then prevent the high

Fig. 4.—METHOD OF RE-ASSEMBLING CLUTCH.

pinion moving whilst the nut and sprocket are being withdrawn.

The sprocket lock nut is fitted to the high-pinion sleeve by a left-hand thread. The high pinion is mounted on cup-and-cone bearings, and is in a double track of 40 $\frac{1}{4}$-inch ball bearings. Adjustment of the high-pinion cones is made by pen-steel shim washers.

Inspecting Parts for Wear

With the box dismantled, thoroughly wash the gears and the inside of the gearbox housing. This will greatly help when examining the gears.

Should the dogs of the pinions become rounded off, then examine the control plate and selector fork, as most probably the latter will be strained and the former distorted.

To ascertain whether the selector fork is strained, take two pieces of straight rod, place one piece between the forked ends of the selector fork, and one piece through the bolt hole in the fork; then by sighting across the two pieces of rod it will be immediately ascertained how much the selector fork is out of alignment. The fork should be reset, whilst the control plate, if worn, be renewed.

Another way to ascertain whether the selector fork is strained is an examination of both the high pinion and mainshaft middle pinion dogs. Should the fork be strained it will be noticed that these dogs have not been engaging to their fullest extent.

All pinions should be replaced with new ones in cases where the corners of the dogs have become rounded off. On no account should these dogs be ground up, as they will break down again in a very short period. There is only one remedy, i.e. to replace all worn parts, as to fit a new pinion to work in conjunction with a worn one is courting disaster.

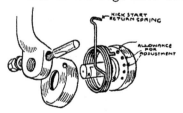

Fig. 5.—KICK-STARTER.

Showing the arrangement of the kick-starter.

This advice also applies to both the main and layshafts, as, should the corners of the splines be damaged, then the internal dogs in the pinions will also be damaged. Replacements are necessary. Should the mainshaft bronze thrust washer be worn, fit a new one.

It is important that the centres of the layshaft ballrace in the gearbox housing and the mainshaft race in the gearbox end cover have not sunk, as this will permit the shafts to float when the centre pinions are being moved. In all probability it will prevent the dogs from engaging as they should do : the remedy for this is to fit new ball journals.

Another point to examine is the kick-starter release cam and rivet. Should these be worn or damaged, fit new ones. Excessive back firing will cause the release cam to become badly worn.

Reassembling

The gearbox should now be assembled in the following manner, after first renewing all worn parts. Place the piece of flat metal plate (used to detach the high pinion when the gearbox was dismantled) vertically in the vice.

High-pinion Bearings—First Set

Assuming that the high-pinion cup has not been removed from the gearbox, proceed to fit the first set of 20 ¼-inch ball bearings round the high-pinion cone : stiff grease will greatly assist in this operation.

Second Set

Hold the high pinion vertically in the right hand, place the housing over the pinion until the sleeve passes through the aperture in the high-pinion cup, then hold the high pinion by the sleeve. Place both gearbox housing and pinion over the piece of steel plate in the vice, and engage the top of the plate with the high-pinion dogs. Fit the second set of ball bearings, slip on the cone, the oil-retaining washer, dust cap and lock nut, tightening the nut.

Adjustment

Should the tightening of the high-pinion lock nut cause the pinion to bind in its bearing when the cones are in position, remove the high-pinion cone last fitted, and fit between the two cones pen-steel shim washers until the bearing is perfectly free with the nut locked up. On the other hand, probably when the box was dismantled there were two or three shim washers fitted. Remove one of these shim washers, which will take up wear and tear of the high-pinion cones and cup.

Sprocket Lock Plate and Pin

Fit the sprocket lock plate and pin. The gearbox should now be placed in the vice by securing the suspension studs between the jaws of the vice, with the open end of the gearbox facing the operator.

Layshaft High Pinion

Proceed to fit the layshaft high pinion to the layshaft. This is fitted with the flat face inwards. Slide the shaft into the ballrace in the housing, at the same time engaging the layshaft high-pinion teeth with those of the mainshaft high pinion, then fit the mainshaft into the high-pinion sleeve ; next the control plate over the two sliding pinions. These pinions are identified in the following manner :

How to identify the Pinions

The teeth on the mainshaft middle pinion come between the dogs and the groove which carries the control plate, whilst with the layshaft pinion the dogs are on the side of the pinion nearest the control plate, also the layshaft pinion is larger in diameter than the mainshaft one.

Slide the pinions, together with the plate, on to their respective shafts. Partly screw into the housing the two selector-fork bushes, then fit the selector fork into position. Hold this whilst the quadrant and selector-fork bolt are fitted into the bushes, then fit the selector-fork bolt nut.

Now place on the mainshaft the low pinion. This pinion is fitted to the mainshaft with the face of the pinion inwards. Should the pinion be fitted in the reverse manner, the gears will be difficult to change, and

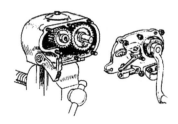

Fig. 6.
Showing the gearbox end cover removed.

trouble will eventually follow. The same remark applies to the high-pinion lay-shaft.

If the gearbox end plate has not already been examined,

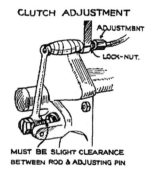

CLUTCH ADJUSTMENT

ADJUSTMENT

LOCK-NUT.

MUST BE SLIGHT CLEARANCE BETWEEN ROD & ADJUSTING PIN

Fig. 7.
Showing the clutch rod adjustment.

it may be found necessary to fit a new kick-starter pawl release cam and rivet. Fit these components, then slide the gearbox end plate into position, but on no account must force be used. If necessary, a thick paper washer should be fitted (three different thicknesses in washers can be obtained from the manufacturers). Should the gearbox be assembled too tightly, then the low-gear kick-starter wheel seizes to the layshaft.

Fit the gearbox end-cover nuts, then the box should be turned in the vice with the clutch side towards the operator.

Refitting Clutch

Fit the woodruff key to the mainshaft, slide the clutch centre into position, taking care that it does not ride on the key. Fit the clutch-centre lock washer, then the locking nut, tightening same securely.

Now fit the clutch back plate and the roller race. A little patience is required to fit this race, but to the practised hand the race will fit quite readily. Next fit the friction disk, the chain ring, friction disk, clutch centre plate, friction disk, clutch friction plate, friction disk, clutch outer plate, clutch thrust plate, clutch spring, clutch spring thrust washer and clutch nut. If difficulty is encountered in fitting the clutch nut, an easy method to do this is to place the nut in position in the thrust washer. Take a short hammer, place the end of the hammer shaft against the chest, then a little pressure will compress the spring, whilst the kick-starter crank should be depressed several times to give the nut a start, when it can be readily tightened up.

With this done, fit the push rod, the clutch end pin and the thrust-cover cap.

When adjusting the clutch, after refitting the gearbox to the machine, see that there is at least $\frac{1}{16}$ inch idle movement between the clutch actuating lever and the push rod.

74

OVERHAUL AND ADJUSTMENT OF RUDGE GEARBOX AND CLUTCH

By B. P. Ransom (*Rudge Whitworth Ltd.*)

THE Rudge four-speed gearbox is an exceedingly compact unit, being in fact no larger than the majority of three-speed boxes. While the overhaul and re-erection of this presents no outstanding difficulties to the experienced mechanic, it can hardly be too strongly emphasised that the best policy that the amateur can follow is to leave well alone. In any case, the box should not be dismantled, except in the very unlikely event of the appearance of definite symptoms of trouble.

Dismantling

The gearbox having been removed from the frame, it should be firmly held in a vice by the two lugs by which it is secured between the cradle plates, and the small sprocket removed. This, since the beginning of 1927, is merely driven on to splines on the fourth speed wheel, and secured in place by a left-hand lock nut. Previous to this date, however, the sprocket was screwed on to the fourth speed wheel with a right-hand thread and locked by a left-hand nut outside. It is exceedingly difficult to remove the sprockets from these old boxes unless one has access to the special jig for the purpose. This jig employs the relative motion between the fourth speed wheel and the mainshaft when the indirect gears are engaged, and is available at the leading agents, as well as at the works.

Important

The next operation is to remove the cover over the operating quadrant. The bush in which this quadrant turns is threaded, and is locked in position by a grub screw. It should be noted that the thread on this bush is a manufacturing adjustment only, and on no account should this be altered. If on re-erection the grub screw is entered in the original hole, and difficulty is experienced in engaging gear or adjusting control, the trouble must be looked for elsewhere.

Next the end cover of the gearbox should be removed. If the nut securing the starter crank be taken off first, the whole of the starter mechanism will come away with the cover, leaving the layshaft spindle in place.

Withdrawing the Gears

The first speed wheel should then be removed from the layshaft, and both the layshaft and mainshaft partially withdrawn. It will then be found possible to pull the mainshaft and layshaft far enough apart to free the striking plates. When these are removed, the remainder of the wheels and shafts can be taken from the box together.

Fig. 1.—Adjusting Clutch Control by Grub Screw in Clutch-operating Lever.

The nut should be locked after the adjustment is taken up by the screw, which is held meanwhile by the screwdriver.

Take Care of Rollers

The greatest of care should be taken to observe the order in which the parts come away, or considerable trouble may be caused when attempting to re-erect the box. In particular, it should be noted that there are three lengths of rollers employed, without counting the race in the kick-starter ratchet carrier.

The longest rollers are fitted inside the fourth speed wheel, in two rows, with a washer in between. The intermediate length is used outside the fourth speed wheel, while the shortest are used inside the pinion on the inside of the layshaft.

Inspecting for Wear

Having dismantled the box, all parts should be washed in paraffin, and examined for wear. Particular attention should be paid to the

Note the pressed steel cover plate has already been taken off. The gear is engaged, and the mainshaft held stationary through rear chain by application of the brake. If the clutch has to be removed single-handed, it would be better to leave the front chain in place, and slacken the nut by a sharp tap with a hammer on the tommy bar against the compression.

Fig. 2.—REMOVING THE CLUTCH CENTRE NUT.

77

ends of the splines on both shafts, and the corresponding female splines in the two pairs of sliding wheels.

If the clutch has not been freeing properly, or if sufficient care has not been given to gear changing, these points will be found to have the corners rounded off, and if the trouble be allowed to develop, the symptom of jumping out of gear may follow. The same remarks apply to the ends of the pegs on the two large sliding wheels, and to the entrance of the corresponding holes in the first and fourth speed wheels. Other points worthy of particular attention are the loose washers behind the fourth and first speed wheels, and at each end of the mainshaft, particularly if symptoms of endplay in the shafts are noticeable.

Types of Operating Quadrants

If it should be necessary to replace the operating quadrant, it is important to note that there are several types in existence which do not differ greatly one from the other. The quadrant in use from 1929 to the present day has the top gear in the back position of the control lever, whereas the 1927 and 1928 quadrant has it forwards. For the previous two years to this, the quadrant had a shorter throw, and the angular position of the gear lever in the various positions deviated from the present type.

In reconditioning a box of this age, then, it must be remembered that while it would be an improvement to fit a 1928 pattern operating quadrant, the control quadrant, if any, must be removed from the tank.

Reassembling

When starting to re-erect the gearbox, first of all pack the fourth speed wheel bearing ring with intermediate size rollers, using good quality vaseline to hold them in place. The fourth speed wheel itself should then be packed with two rows of the long rollers with the separating washer in between. Place the fourth speed wheel in the box. Next, arrange the two pairs of sliding wheels on the mainshaft and layshaft, the pegs for the drive towards the clutch end of the mainshaft, and of course the reverse direction on the layshaft. The mainshaft should next be entered in the fourth speed wheel, not forgetting the washer, but should not be pushed home. The striking plates should be placed in the groove of the two sliding wheels on the mainshaft and engaged with the slots in the striking forks. Then pack the short rollers in the layshaft, using vaseline as before, and push the layshaft spindle through. The layshaft complete should then be put in the box, and as in dismantling, the two shafts should then be held apart to enable the striking plates to enter the grooves in the layshaft sliding wheels. Both shafts should now be pushed home. The first speed wheel, washer and roller race on the end of the layshaft and the mainshaft washer are next put in place, and the gearbox cover can then be replaced, provided that the kick-starter mechanism has not been disturbed.

Fig. 3.—THE CLUTCH COMPLETE REMOVED FROM THE GEARBOX MAINSHAFT.

Assembling Kick-starter

If this has, however, been taken down, care must be taken to assemble correctly, or the ratchet teeth may fail to clear each other, which will of course cause rapid wear, to say nothing of noise.

The correct procedure is as follows : the kick-starter carrier should be placed on its bearing and the two ends of the return spring hooked in place. The crank should next be wound up until it has passed the vertical. The crank should then be pushed on to its serrations. Next, the ratchet-drive sleeve and spring should be threaded on the quick pitch thread on the carrier in such a position that when the stop lug on the driving sleeve comes into contact with the stop on the gearbox cover, the crank inclines to the rear of the machine at an angle of about 20°.

Always Remember

It is essential that the gearbox is adequately lubricated, and that it is periodically inspected to see that the level of oil is maintained. Engine oil such as Castrol XXL is quite suitable, and the low position of the filler cap prevents overfilling.

When filling the gearbox it will be found of assistance to slip the cable from the end of the clutch operating lever and fold the latter right back. This will give easy access to the filler plug. When adjusting the front chain, do not forget that it is necessary to adjust the gear control. If the machine be placed on the stand, and the rear wheel rocked to and fro, an adjustment of the rod can be found, which will make the position of the lever relative to the end of the gate the same in top and bottom gears.

Adjusting Gear Control

If the gear control rod is observed to spring and bottom gear is difficult to engage, although the adjustment seems correct, examine the fork joint at the bottom of the rod. This may be fouling the lever on the operating quadrant, and may be eased with a touch of a file. These last remarks also apply to top gear in the 1928 and previous models.

And Clutch

There are two points at which the clutch control may be adjusted. One is the screwed cable adjuster, threaded into the arm cast on the gearbox cover, and the other is the grub screw in the clutch operating lever (Fig. 1). It is advisable to use the former as a running adjustment to take up cable stretch, as if the grub screw be used for the purpose it will soon be working at such an angle that excessive side thrust is thrown on the two push rods. These push rods, by the way, should periodically be removed, inspected for wear, and be well greased before being replaced. The cable should be so adjusted that a perceptible amount of play can be felt at the handlebar control lever, otherwise clutch slip will result.

Dismantling Clutch

To remove the clutch from the gearbox first of all remove the pressed steel cover plate, bend back the locking tab from the central nut, and slacken off this latter a few turns (Fig. 2). A sharp blow with a hammer on the nut will then probably release the clutch on the taper (Fig. 3). If it does not do so an extractor screwing on to the clutch centre with a set screw bearing on the mainshaft end must be used. We do not advise the overhaul of clutches away from the factory. If, however, it is desired to take this unit to pieces, it should be carried out either in place on the gearbox, or on an old mainshaft securely held in a vice. The cover plate having been removed, the steering-head " C " spanner should be placed in such a position that it bridges the central nut, but bears against two opposite spring boxes. The necessary leverage to unscrew the spring plate may be obtained by slipping a piece of tube over the handle of the spanner.

A Special Tool

If the spanner shows any tendency to bend, a sturdier tool may be made from a strip of steel $\frac{3}{16} \times 1\frac{1}{4}$ inches. A gap should be cut in the side of this $1\frac{1}{4}$ inches long and $\frac{5}{8}$ inch deep to bridge the nut, and the strip inserted between the spring boxes as above.

As soon as the spring plate is removed the successive members of the clutch can be taken off one at a time, the greatest care being taken that the order in which they come off is noted, so that they may be correctly replaced.

SCOTT GEARBOX AND CLUTCH

By J. H. KELLY (*Scott Motors Ltd.*)

SCOTT TWO-SPEED GEAR

THIS is removed quite easily from the frame as follows : Disconnect kick-starter chain from rear end, take out hollow bolt in left-hand gear lug, remove footrests (for "freedom"), rear chain, gear pedal, sleeve nut and washer, outer drum and strap, washers on shaft (note the order in which they come off), undo ⅜-inch shaft nut and remove inner drum, lift up gear, take off kick-starter device complete, and slip off chains ; drop gear through bottom of frame (see Fig. 1).

Dismantling Gear

Undo slotted ring on ratchet side (right-hand thread), lift off high gear drum, expanding ring, distance washer and ball cage. Take out two pivoting screws in the thrust lever (you will note locking washers on these : when replacing screws always fit new washers), lift off thrust lever, low gear drum, ring distance washer and ball cage.

Take off locking ring at driving end (also right-hand thread), lift off sprocket (located by two flats on the hub). Cones are accessible, take off cone at *this end first*. As the cups are a drive-in fit, a light tap on the hollow shaft (insert hollow bolt a few threads first) will carry out the whole spindle centre thrust and cup complete (Fig. 2).

Centre Thrust

The two large nuts and thrust washers are threaded on to the sleeve (right-hand thread), and should any of the washer cages, the sleeve or the thrust block itself show signs of pitting or wear, fit new parts. (The sleeve is riveted through the hollow shaft to the solid spindle.)

Reassembly

The sleeve *must* work freely on the spindle ; see that no play is allowed on the centre thrust and main bearings, but that all run freely ; thin steel washers are supplied for cone adjustment (short end of shaft) to allow the cones to be tightened up against the shoulders of the shaft. (*Note.*— There are 50 balls, $\frac{9}{32}$ inch, in the gear, 24 in the thrust assembly and 26 in the main cups, even number each side.) SPECIAL NOTE.— Put the balls back loosely ; DON'T use grease to " place " them ; this only blocks up the oilways and causes trouble.

Lubricate Drums with Paraffin

The quick thread drums should be lubricated with paraffin only and the strap adjusted carefully, as this makes a deal of difference in the sweetness of engagement; if both gears slip unless you have your foot on the pedal, this proves that the strap is too slack, so tighten up slightly. Don't put too much pressure on the sleeve nut when tightening — remember it is only a $\frac{1}{4}$-inch thread, and very easily broken off.

Fig. 1.—How the Gear drops through the Frame when Dismantling.

The thin $\frac{1}{4}$-in. washers on the thrust rod are for pedal adjustment: increasing the number will engage *low* gear with *less* movement of pedal, and decreasing the number will allow the pedal to go down *farther* into low gear, high gear being affected accordingly (Fig. 6.) Oversize rollers are supplied to take up wear, but don't rush to these immediately ; remember that play on the cones or centre thrust (an excessive amount of neutral on the gear pedal usually indicates this) will be taken up by the *whole gear moving bodily*, before the rollers enter the drums.

Fig. 2.—REMOVING THRUST ASSEMBLY FROM GEAR HUB.

Insert a hollow bolt for a few threads. A light tap on the bolt will drive out the assembly.

Sideplay on the gear drums (up to $\frac{1}{16}$ inch permissible) can be taken up by means of a slightly thicker side plate distance washer.

Changing Gear Ratios (Two Speed)

This can be done by changing the sprocket fitted to the hub flange on the outside (19-, 20-, 21-, and 22-teeth sprockets are supplied).

These sprockets are held on the flange by a lock ring (right-hand thread) and a set screw (also right-hand). On unscrewing these, the sprocket may be removed and another replaced.

See that the locking ring and set screw are *tight* when replaced.

It is not necessary to take the gear out of the frame for this job ; remove locking ring and screw, take out hollow bolt and distance washer and sprocket can be removed. When replacing the hollow bolt, take care that you do not cross the threads.

SCOTT KICK-STARTER

This is of course a separate unit from the gear itself, and can be removed without taking out the gear, as follows :

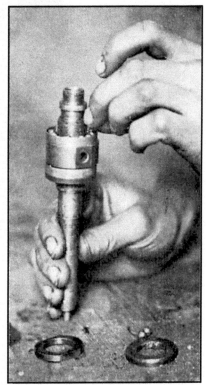

Fig. 3.—PLACING BALLS IN CENTRE THRUST.

Don't use grease to " place " them.

Detach chain from rod, take off gear pedal and drums, slacken off left-hand gear lug clamping bolt and gear chain adjuster nuts, undo gear oil pipe ; gear can then be tilted and the kick-starter pulled off.

When refitting, take out sparking plugs to allow engine to rotate easily, slide kick-starter on shaft, refit gear into frame. (*Note.*—See that the two small pins on the back of the inner quick thread drum fit snugly into the slots in the gear lug, otherwise difficulty will be found in getting the gear pedal adjustment correct.)   Attach a piece of cord to the chain, wind round ratchet about 1⅓ turns (clockwise), bringing loose end to

Fig. 4.—How to locate Thrust Lever Screws.

rear ; engage high gear and pull cord, turning rear wheel forward, until chain anchor is within ⅛ of a revolution from top.

Hold ratchet in position with a screwdriver wedged between it and frame, attach starter chain to rod, withdraw screwdriver (Fig. 5).

Just one warning here.—On no account turn the rear wheel backwards, as this will damage the spring.

Adjustment of rod and chain is made by the link at the end of the rod (attached to the lever), and in rest position the ratchets should be just clear of each other.   If you find that no amount of adjustment will clear ratchets, remove kick-starter and fit one or more thin gear cone washers between the ratchets on the shaft ; this will then throw them clear of each other.

If the kick-starter sticks at the end of the stroke, this may be due to dirt or want of oil. Clean out thoroughly with petrol, and give copious supplies of oil ; failing that, it is possible that the small 2 B.A. nut holding the chain eye on the ratchet drum has become loose and has turned round, fouling the gear lug on the down stroke. This nut should be riveted over and filed flush with the edge of the drum to prevent this.

SCOTT THREE-SPEED GEARBOX

This requires little attention above the usual oiling, but we will dismantle for safety.

Remove kick-starter screw and cap and hold the spring with a pair of pliers, pull it off the pin, release spring. Take off kick-starter cap (the notched one), *left-hand* thread, and kick-starter stop by detaching sleeve nut. Then kick-starter itself will pull off by rotating in a forward

Fig. 5.—Connecting up Kick-starter Chain.

After giving spring a full turn, jamb screwdriver between gear lug and device to hold in position.

direction until the pawl " rides " on the boss.

The ratchet bolt and washer can now be removed (right-hand thread) and ratchet taken off its square ; now take out the three remaining cover sleeve nuts.

A smart tap on the end of the mainshaft will break the cover joint (assuming that the sprocket housing has been taken off, of course) ; continue tapping the shaft and the end of gearbox will come off with the middle- and low-gear wheel assembly. Assuming that the " innards " *don't* come out with the cover, withdraw layshaft, slip off middle- and low-gear wheel assembly from mainshaft. Mainshaft can then be withdrawn, which will allow sliding dog to fall free; take care that you collect the small fork shoes, which may drop out of the fork.

High-gear wheel can only be removed after clutch is dismantled. When reassembling, be sure that all parts and joints are perfectly clean, making cover joint with Metalastine.

Fig. 6.—ORDER. OF GEAR-PEDAL WASHERS.

Plain ¼-inch washer is on shaft and ⅜-inch double-coil washer in hand ready to put on. Ordinary ⅜-inch spring washer and sleeve nut are put on after outer drum is fitted.

THE SCOTT CLUTCH

How to Dismantle

This can be dismantled, if required, without disturbing the gearbox by just removing the sprocket housing and rear chain and then carrying on as follows :

Remove hexagon nuts (or screws, according to type) and clutch springs (6), and the whole clutch body and plates will come away together. Take care that none of the race rollers (30 Flyer and Super) fall out and get lost.

If you wish to get at the clutch operation worm, take off race-plate locking nut (the edge of its locking washer must be prised off the flat face of the nut first), pull off race plate, then the ball-thrust race, washer, clutch worm lever and spring.

Should the thrust washer be worn this may be reversed, as may also the corresponding washer which is fitted *in* the lever itself, these being case hardened ; if they are pitted, reverse at once, as once this has started it will wear quickly, with the result that a lot of waste movement is set up on the lever before the thrust pins touch the outer plate and " clutch drag " sets in.

Reassembling the Scott Clutch

When reassembling, be sure that the race-plate nut is tight and the locking washer turned over. It will be as well to note the condition of the felt washer inside this nut, as if this is hard or perished, oil will tend to creep along the mainshaft and cause clutch slip (i.e. if gearbox is too generously filled).

The order of plates is as follows : (1) small plate ; (2) plate with inserts, two similar groups, then the outer plate. Springs should be replaced, tightening them in pairs diametrically opposite each other ; lock the nuts by split pins or a length of copper wire.

Don't burn Oil off Inserts

If at any time you wish to examine plates without taking gearbox out of frame, make sure that you hold the clutch body in position (if solo, lean machine over on right-hand footrest), in order that the rollers do not drop out from their cage. If you get clutch slip through oil-saturated inserts (this may happen if you overfill the gearbox, which by the way should only be filled up to the oil boss plug, about half-way up on the gearbox cover), let the plates soak in petrol for a few minutes, brush vigorously and " rough up " with a file. DON'T BURN THE OIL OFF, this only buckles the plates and swells the inserts ; if you think the inserts too bad or worn, replace one plate (next the *outer* plate) with new inserts (about three shillings worth).

Just another point : it may be advisable, after many thousands of miles' wear on the inserts, to grind the thrust pins down a little, but these *must* be done evenly, otherwise you will get a " cockeyed " action and clutch drag, but on relining the plates with *new* inserts you must fit standard pins (the others of course being now too short).

On Supers

If the plates get too saturated, fit four new Ferodo linings, putting one of these immediately behind the race plate, and if clutch tends to slip under heavy sidecar work, put a thin washer under each of the six springs (this tensions them a little), although this will necessarily make the clutch a little " heavier " in action.

Lengthening the Life of Clutch Wires

Many people consider that the heavier the clutch cable the longer the life. Well, this may be, but a light clutch wire does not necessarily mean a short life—what it does mean is a really light action. The writer has

Fig. 7.—LIFTING UP PAWL SPRING.
To replace pawl which has jumped out after violent backfire.

the original light clutch wire on his Flyer and sidecar—used quite a lot
in London traffic (Londoners will appreciate this point !)—which has
seen nearly eighteen months' service. There is nothing wonderful about
this, and the secret (if you can call it such) is a $\frac{5}{16}$-inch round nipple at
the top end which *floats* in the lever, i.e. not jammed in, as, sad to relate,
we see so many, cable oiled frequently (particularly at the adjuster,
half-way along the cable), and the top nipple and first few inches of
inner wire *thoroughly greased* periodically against the rain rust.

Alter Gear Ratios when Fitting Sidecar

The gear ratio can be changed in about twenty minutes, by taking off
the sprocket housing complete, remove end plate which screws out,
unscrew sprocket lock nut, and tap out sprocket from ballrace—refit new
sprocket by reversing process.

Scott Kick-starter Trouble

If this slips it is usually due to dirt on the pawl or broken ratchet
teeth ; in any case, it is a matter of minutes to take it to pieces and examine.
Worn pawls or ratchets should be replaced. If, after a backfire, the kick-
starter slips, you will find that the pawl has " jumped " from under the
long clip spring around the kick-starter body ; lift this spring up with a
screwdriver and replace pawl. The spring will automatically press pawl
back into engagement (see Fig. 7).

THE STURMEY-ARCHER GEARBOX

By T. L. WILLIAMS and S. A. NEWTON

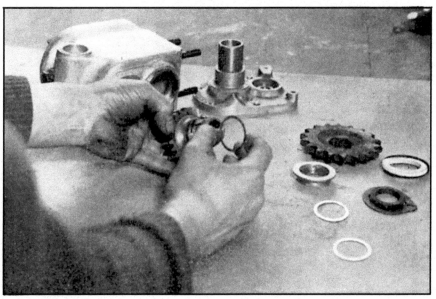

Fig. 1.—WASHERS USED FOR ADJUSTING THE DOUBLE BALL BEARINGS WHICH SUPPORT THE MAIN GEAR WHEEL.

MAINTENANCE ATTENTIONS

IT might be claimed that the gearbox should be used but not heard, but it will be appreciated that if this desirable feature is to be maintained, it will be necessary to remember its presence and regularly give that little attention which it deserves.

Lubrication

It is, for instance, essential that all the internals receive correct lubrication. The gears are not greedy in this respect, but in cases where the machine is not used for a long period, say during the winter months, it should be remembered that the oil or grease is likely to gradually drain from the upper half. The practice of running the engine slowly so as to circulate the grease for a few seconds and keep all bearings covered against

*Fig. 2.—*THE GEARS AND SHAFTS.

The dog clutches and splines have been marked to show those which engage to provide each of the three ratios.

rust is not practised as often as it should be. The fact that the box contains lubricant does not ensure that all the parts are immune from damage when such precautions are neglected.

Check Nuts Periodically

During use we must also be prepared to guard against lost nuts due to vibration. Spring washers or other locking devices are always fitted where possible, but it is also worth while going over all nuts occasionally to make sure they have not worked loose.

EXTERNAL ADJUSTMENTS

Gear Controls

Adjustments will usually be confined to the external fittings, and quite simple tests will generally indicate any need for attention. The gear control on modern machines can hardly alter of its own accord, though on older models it may be necessary to see that clamping bolts do not work loose. The moving parts of all controls also need lubrication, and vaseline or a fairly stiff grease is often preferable to oil for this purpose. It is not wise to use too much, because this will collect mud and grit, besides tending to get on to one's clothes. Do not forget the spindles round which the various levers work, nor the little swivels which connect the ends of the control rods to the levers. All these points must also be watched for wear, because as soon as any appreciable play develops, the movement which the controls should impart to the dog clutches inside the box will be lessened, and if the dogs are not pulled into full engagement, there will naturally be a tendency for them to slip out again.

When adjusting or fitting Chains

It is chiefly when the gearbox has to be moved in order to adjust the front chain that the gear control rod has to be altered in length. Assuming that the box has been slid backwards the rod must be lengthened. Remove the split pin and washer and the swivel pin which connects the gear control lever with its rod, and unscrew the connection one or two turns on the rod. If the gears are indexed internally it is easy to engage middle gear before removing this pin, and then merely adjust the top connection piece until its holes for the pin register correctly with the pin hole in the lever, so that the pin slides easily into position without any force being applied.

Adjusting Early Models

In earlier gears, where internal indexing is not adopted, the pin must be slipped in and the gears tested from the neutral position. Move the lever towards low gear, turning the back wheel to and fro all the time, and note how far it moves before you can feel the dogs just grating across each other. Then go back to neutral and move the lever towards middle gear. If the adjustment is correct the lever will move the same distance on each side before the dogs commence to engage. It is not necessary to add the washer and split pin until the correct setting has been found.

Adjusting Clutch Control

The clutch control also should be regularly checked and oiled. It is not easily possible to lubricate the Bowden wire inside its cable, but whenever a new one is fitted be sure that it is carefully greased *before* it is passed through the cable, and very little attention will afterwards be necessary. The handlebar lever must be kept free, and the security of its attachment should also be checked occasionally. Where a worm and nut operation is used at the gearbox end of the wire, the anchorage of the Bowden wire stop should always be free to swivel. This stop stud screws into the gearbox cover, but it is *not* intended that it should be screwed up tight.

Taking up Slack Cable

All Bowden cable wires are liable to stretch, and the clutch wire is probably subjected to a greater strain than the other similar controls commonly used on motor-cycles. The usual means of adjustment are provided, and it is better to rely upon the stop screw than to reset the worm lever on the worm, or to adjust the screw in the so-called direct-pull type of operating lever. It is always advisable that the lever should be as nearly vertical as possible when it takes the load of the clutch spring. With a direct-pull lever the adjusting screw should also be exactly in line with the clutch rod for best results and not pushing at an angle.

WEAR IN THE CLUTCH

We can now turn our attention to the wearing parts. First of all comes the *clutch*. Everyone will recognise that sooner or later the very act of letting in the clutch will result in the friction inserts wearing down. As this happens the outer plate will bed down nearer to the box, the clutch rod passing through the axle will become relatively too long, and the clutch control wire may possibly have to be lengthened slightly to avoid the clutch being prevented from engaging properly. This means that the tension of the clutch spring or springs will be less effective until eventually the clutch will begin to slip.

We must, however, watch that the inserts do not wear so low as to allow the metal of the plate in which they are fitted to come into contact with the plain steel plate on either side. This can sometimes happen before the slipping commences, and should therefore be guarded against.

Fig. 3.—Removing the Gearbox Cover, and parting the Oilproof Joint Washer.

Fitting new Inserts

New inserts can be fitted to the plates. Sometimes corks are used and sometimes an asbestos fibre composition, of which, perhaps, the best known is Ferodo. Corks can be fitted fairly easily by hand, especially if they are first soaked in hot water. Then, when dry, lay the plate flat on a large sheet of glass paper and rub gently up and down to obtain a perfectly even surface. Ferodo or similar inserts can also be fitted by hand, but they require flattening out afterwards to secure them, and it is not easy to ensure a good flat face by hammering them out one by one. The gearbox makers have special presses for this work, and it is best to send the plates to them whenever it is possible, even if it means keeping a spare set of plates on hand.

HOW TO DISMANTLE THE CLUTCH

Instructions for dismantling clutches are given in the booklets provided free to all owners by the Sturmey-Archer Gears, Ltd., and these details are copied below.

Single-spring Clutches

First unscrew the clutch end cap, C.S. 173A. If a special spanner is not available use a hammer and a punch for this purpose. It has a right-hand thread, and must be unscrewed in an anti-clockwise direction.

Fig. 4.—Two Spanners are here being used to remove the Clutch Centre from the Mainshaft. Rather Thicker Wedges will be necessary in some Cases where a Wider Engine Chain Line is Employed.

The clutch adjuster nut is then exposed, and should be unscrewed, bearing in mind that it also has a right-hand thread. Remove clutch spring with the collar, and then the spring cup. The plates can now be withdrawn, noting particularly the direction in which the dished centre portions of these face, as they vary, and it is essential that they are replaced exactly as they were found originally. With these points carefully noted there should be no difficulty in reassembling. If the inserts are fairly thin, but otherwise in good condition, one of the washers used under the clutch adjuster nut may be removed in order to obtain additional spring tension ; also be sure the end cap is screwed up thoroughly tight.

Multi-spring Clutches

The six screws which hold the clutch springs should be unscrewed first, afterwards lifting out the springs and spring boxes. The spring box plate and the other clutch plates are then lifted apart, as described for the central spring clutches. No adjustment of the spring tension is provided, but extra strong springs are available in case of need. We do not recommend fitting these unless absolutely essential, as they are inclined to make the clutch more difficult to release.

Shock-absorber Clutches

The clutch portion can be dismantled as described for the plain type. The shock absorber may present some difficulty, as the screws holding the parts together are burred over, to prevent the lock nuts from working loose. After the four screws have been removed, the driver can be withdrawn, and the rubbers taken out of the slots in the body of the sprocket. The positions of the rubbers should be carefully noted. The solid rubbers are fitted in the driving side, and those with the small hole on the opposite side. To dismantle the bearing on the central spring type, remove the split ring and the washer behind it. The sprocket can now be taken off the centre. To remove the sprocket from the bearing in the multi-spring type, it is necessary to unscrew the six nuts on the clutch-spring studs. The small plate and the sprocket can then be removed. The sprocket bearing in the clutches is composed of loose $\frac{1}{4}$-inch diameter balls and rollers placed alternately. These should be assembled with grease.

Examine Clutch Drum Slots

If your clutch is fierce, or if you engage it suddenly, you may cause the tongues of the clutch friction plates to wear grooves in the slots of the flange in which they slide. These grooves will then prevent the plates sliding as easily and freely as they should, making it both difficult to release the clutch, and causing the re-engagement to become jerky. If the clutch sticks out, suspect this cause. The grooves can be filed away, but this is only a temporary relief, because the tongues will no longer fit snugly and the backlash allowed will cause the same wear to occur again fairly soon. You may also burr up the edges of the tongues on the plates in this way and so cause more expense.

If the Clutch is Stiff to Operate

Should stiffness develop in releasing the clutch, it is first necessary to make sure none of the strands of the control wire have broken or become rusty. In the case of the worm and nut type of control, examine the worn threads on both parts for wear, and adjust the lever on the worm to ensure that it is nearly vertical when commencing to release the plates, shortening the wire if necessary to suit, and make sure that the clutch rod inside the axle has not worn short.

Examine for Endplay

There is one gear fault that will make the clutch difficult to withdraw, namely, a floating movement of the axle from end to end of the box. Since the clutch is secured to the end of the axle, this movement has to be taken up before it is possible to start separating the clutch plates. This limits the movement of the clutch rod, which is available for releasing the clutch, and may make it impossible to obtain a perfectly free clutch. The reasons for this end movement are explained under the heading " Wear of the Gear Parts."

WEAR OF THE GEAR PARTS

How to avoid Premature Wear

It is better not to wait for some tendency of one of the gears to slip out of mesh to warn one that the gears are in need of attention. The heaviest load is applied by the weight of the clutch plus the pull of the chains on the mainshaft. This shaft passes right through the main gear wheel on all Sturmey-Archer gearboxes, and a long plain bearing occurs between these two parts. This bearing needs adequate lubrication, and it is one of the most vulnerable parts to suffer if the machine is laid up for any long period. If this happens, before taking the model on the road again, inject two or three teaspoonfuls of thin oil, and lean the machine over on the clutch side with the engine running slowly. If this thin oil will penetrate along the oil grooves on the axle, the thicker lubricant recommended for general use will follow later, but if the bearing is once allowed to become dry, the ordinary grease in the box will not work its way along. The only remedy then is to completely dismantle everything and smear the axle with grease before reassembling.

Testing Main Bearing

When the axle wears thinner or the main gear-wheel bore wears larger, you will be able to move the clutch up and down to the extent of the play allowed. But in this test it must also be remembered that if the main gear wheel is slack in its own bearings, the clutch can be lifted to this extent over and above the play existing in the plain bearing. The main gear-wheel bearings consist of a double cup and cone arrangement, and the two cones on the gear wheel are renewable. Also a few thin adjusting washers are used between them, so that if the bearing surfaces remain in good condition, you can remove these washers one at a time, so bringing the cones very slightly closer together to adjust the bearing exactly. This, of course, involves completely dismantling everything, and is probably a job the average amateur will prefer to place in practical hands, but it should never be neglected, as it is likely to cause more serious trouble if allowed to develop.

Result of Worn Main Bearings

The up-and-down movement of the clutch is unlikely to cause any running troubles unless it is excessive. If, however, it is due to slackness in the main gear-wheel bearings, it will be

Fig. 5.—The Kick-starter Parts, with the Pawl which revolves the Low Gear Wheel just disengaged from the Cam, which depresses it when the Crank returns to Rest. The Lower "Cam" is the Stop which prevents the Crank and Axle from going back too far and letting the Pawl into engagement again.

accompanied by in-and-out movement on both sprockets. This implies movement of the high gear dogs, and is likely to cause some difficulty in engaging top gear. It also allows the axle to slide to the same extent, and this affects the middle gear and the clutch operation.

Endplay—Cause and Effect

Between the main gear wheel and the splines on the axle a thrust washer is fitted. This slips over a small peg in the axle, and so cannot revolve round the axle. It takes the weight of the clutch spring whenever the clutch is held out, and it will in time wear thin. Then the axle has a further chance to move sideways, helping the middle gear to slip out, and again interfering with the clutch withdrawal. Whilst the wear is only slight, an extra washer may be inserted between the ball bearing and the clutch nut in the gearbox cover. When the clutch nut is screwed up again the ball bearing will be forced inwards a little and take up this slackness. There should be only a just perceptible movement, but we must guard against over-adjustment, which would cause overload of the main gear-wheel bearings. This is harmful, of course.

Carefully Examine

For the rest we can only test the shafts for straightness and look for wear by rounding of the various dog clutches. It is to be understood that the splines on both shafts are included in this term, and we also include the splines along the internal bore of both sliding pinions. We indicate below the dog clutches involved in the case of each gear, and then we must describe how to dismantle the box for inspection.

Top Gear.—Main gear wheel and outer dogs on axle sliding pinion.

Middle Gear.—Inner splines on both sliding pinions and the splines on both shafts.

Low Gear.—Outer dogs on layshaft sliding pinion and slots in kick-starter wheel.

In the case of any broken teeth, always suspect that the shafts may be bent, and see that they are tested and proved straight before using them again. Also if teeth on only one wheel have broken, be very careful to examine the pinion which meshes with those teeth, and make quite sure that it is safe to use it again before attempting to do so.

TO DISMANTLE THE BOX

First disconnect the clutch control wire, and if the gear control operates through the gearbox cover, disconnect the control rod at its lower end. Then remove the cover nuts and gently pull off the cover plate. There are spring washers over each cover stud, so be careful not to lose these. Also do not use a screwdriver or anything similar to part the joint, or oil will leak at this point when reassembled. If the plate sticks, it can usually be removed by one or two light blows with a mallet on the back of the kick-starter crank. The low-gear pinion can be pulled off the mainshaft (it is a push fit over the splined end), and then the complete layshaft and pinions, together with the sliding gear plate and the axle sliding pinion can be lifted out. It may be needless to remove the fork, but if desired the nut which locks the rocking shaft lever should now be unscrewed and the lever withdrawn. Unscrew the bush from the opposite side of the box and knock out the spindle. Always hold a piece of brass or hard wood against threaded parts to prevent damage to the threads when knocking out.

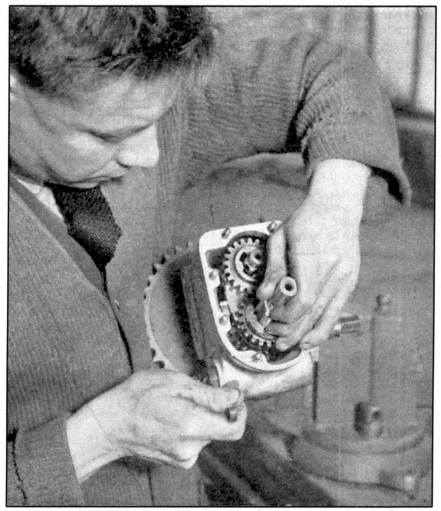

Fig. 6.—How the Lay Shaft and both Sliding Pinions are fitted into Position together. Note how the Pegs on the Sliding Gearplate are being engaged with the Slots in the Operating Fork.

Now turn to the clutch, and dismantle according to instructions already given. To remove the clutch centre from the axle, insert two steel wedges behind it, between that part and the rear drive sprocket. A couple of screwdrivers will do. Tap these in until wedged. Remove the nut and lock washer from the axle. Then hold a piece of brass or hard wood against the axle end, and give one or two sharp blows with a hammer. The brass is merely to protect the screw thread. If this does not loosen the centre, tap in the wedges a little tighter and try again. You can then remove the screws, securing the locking plate on the rear-drive sprocket, and unscrew the sprocket lock nut. Pull off the sprocket, which is a push fit over six splines, and knock the main gear wheel into the shell. In doing this you will release twenty balls $\frac{1}{4}$ inch in diameter from each side of the ball cup in the shell, so be careful not to lose these.

The Kick-starter Parts

First examine the ratchet teeth inside the kick-starter wheel, which is also the low-gear wheel on the layshaft. Then look at the nose of the pawl in the kick-starter axle. It will be best to remove the crank and drop the kick-starter axle from the gearbox cover for examination. It will then be possible to make sure that the pawl plunger and spring are working properly, and that the pin on which the pawl swivels is not broken. If any damage is revealed here, see also that the walls of the kick-starter axle on each side of the pawl are not cracked. Also see that the cam in the box cover depresses the pawl correctly when the kick-starter axle is revolved in the cover.

Reassembling

Fit up the main gear wheel first after setting one row of balls in grease. Set up the other row of balls on their cone, and slip this into position, not forgetting the adjusting washers that go between the cones. Fix the rear drive sprocket and tighten up its lock nut. Then test to see that the main bearings are correctly adjusted and revolve freely but with no shake. If there is shake you must remove one of the washers from between the cones so that the cones can come closer together.

Now fit up the sliding gear fork. Then smear the axle with grease, pass it through the main gear wheel (with thrust washer in position, of course) and assemble the clutch.

The layshaft and its sliding pinion, assembled with the sliding gear plate and axle sliding pinion, are next fitted as one unit, and by holding the end of the layshaft in one hand and the rocking-shaft lever in the other, you can move the fork over to receive the sliding gear plate correctly, and drop all these parts into position together. There is now only the low-gear pinion to push on the end of the mainshaft and the kick-starter wheel to add. Reassemble the kick-starter axle and crank to the box cover, and these should fall into position without any straining.

Early Models—Important Note

One last word regarding the kick-starter. In older models an external stop spring is relied upon to prevent the pawl passing the cam which depresses it. This spring may give, if subject to much backfiring, and if it does the pawl comes into action again and forces the crank forwards, sometimes breaking a footboard. Therefore keep a watchful eye on this spring, and do not omit to renew it if necessary.

REPAIR AND MAINTENANCE OF VELOCETTE GEARBOX

By A. E. FIELD (*Veloce Ltd.*)

THE gearboxes on both two-stroke and four-stroke machines are similar in design, so that the instructions on dismantling and reassembly apply to both types.

It is not advisable to remove the gearbox from the machine until it is dismantled, owing to the difficulty that may be experienced in holding it.

REMOVE THE CHAIN COVERS AND REAR DRIVING CHAIN

Removing Kick-starter

Screw out the drain plug at the bottom of the gearbox housing and drain out the oil. The kick-starter crank should now be removed by unscrewing the nut on the crank cotter and driving the latter out of position with a soft metal punch and a hammer. On early machines the return spring for the kick-starter is of the wire type, and can be removed after unscrewing the small retaining screw. On later models a clock type of spring is used, and after the crank cotter has been withdrawn the crank should be rotated twice in a clockwise direction to release the tension of the spring. The crank can now be withdrawn from the kick-starter shaft complete with spring and spring cover.

How the End Cover is taken off

Unscrew the brass cap covering the end of the gearshaft in the gearbox end cover by unscrewing in an anticlockwise direction. This exposes the nut on the end of the gearshaft, which should be removed with a box spanner as shown in Fig. 1. This nut has an ordinary right-hand thread. The end-cover bolts can now be removed and the end cover withdrawn. If it appears to be held tightly by the ballrace on the end of the layshaft, apply *gentle* leverage, but be very careful not to damage either the housing or end cover. If the end cover will not pull off the kick-starter shaft it is probable that the shaft is bruised, due to incorrect fitting of the crank cotter. In this case the shaft should be eased slightly with fine emery cloth or an oilstone.

Having removed the end cover take off the secondary drive chain and withdraw the split cotter from the sprocket lock nut. Unscrew the lock nut in an anticlockwise direction. On the two-stroke models no split cotter is fitted, security being provided by two lock nuts, both having ordinary right-hand threads.

Dismantling the Gears

The low gear and the layshaft, complete with kick-starter mechanism, can then be lifted out of position as shown in Fig. 2. The mainshaft can then be pulled out from the clutch side, after which the middle gear is free to be removed. The outside striking or selector lever is removable by taking off one nut from the selector spindle in the case of early models, while with later machines it is only necessary to slacken the nut of the pinch bolt, when the lever can be pulled off the square end of the spindle. The selector with spindle and fork can then be withdrawn from the spindle bush in the housing.

Detaching Clutch Complete

To remove the sleeve gear the clutch must be removed, and this is done by unscrewing the sleeve-gear lock nut (this has the appearance of a circular ring with four holes in it, and can be clearly seen in Fig. 3) in an anticlockwise direction. Remove the two thin metal washers and clutch springs to prevent them being lost. The primary driving chain should now be removed by unfastening the spring link. The clutch complete can now be withdrawn from the splines of the sleeve gear in one unit. Remove the three small thrust pins from the holes in the back plate to prevent them being lost. The thrust race, which comprises a washer having a spherical seating, ballrace, plain thrust washer and distance tube, can now be removed from the sleeve gear.

Disconnecting Clutch Control

At this stage the clutch control cable should be detached. The method of detaching from the clutch operating lever on early models is quite obvious. On later models the clutch cable enters the top of the gearbox housing, and can be detached as follows: slack off the lock nut of the adjusting thimble and screw the latter down a little way into the housing. The slotted stop for the outer casing can then be pulled out of position, after which the thimble with lock nut should be unscrewed and pushed up the outer casing of the cable. The cable nipple and top of the operating rod are then exposed, and it only remains to slide the nipple out of the hole in the rod.

The clutch thrust cup can now be taken from the operating lever in the case of early models, or with later types is detached by removing the wire hinge clip.

The sleeve gear can now be pushed out of its bearing from the outside of the gearbox, when the housing can be removed from the machine.

The Layshaft

Turning to the layshaft, the cam should be lifted from the end of the kick-starter shaft and the rollers and springs withdrawn. The shaft can now be driven out of the layshaft with the aid of a lead hammer or rawhide mallet on the o.h.c. models. It should be quite free in the case of the two-stroke machine.

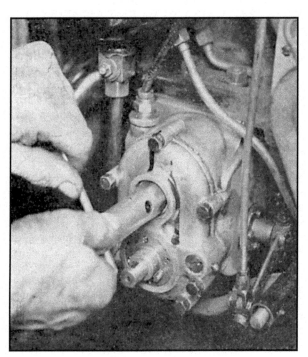

Fig. 1.—REMOVING GEARBOX END COVER.

Unscrewing the nut from the end of the gearbox mainshaft with a box or tube spanner.

Dismantling Clutch

The clutch plates should then be taken apart by lifting off the various plates in the case of the o.h.c. machine, and by lifting off the front plate and chain wheel in the case of the two-stroke models. On the early two-stroke machines the clutch chain wheel is supported on the bearing of the back plate by $\frac{3}{16}$-inch ball bearings, and care should be taken to prevent these being lost when dismantling.

All the parts should now be thoroughly cleaned and the inserts of the clutch plates washed with clean petrol.

Inspecting Parts for Wear

The parts are now ready for examination. Should the sleeve gear ballrace show considerable wear it is desirable to replace it. It is held in position in the housing by a screwed ring, which also acts as a cam for the clutch operating lever on early models. It can be removed by screwing in an anticlockwise direction. It will be noticed that a thin metal shim is present on each side of the ballrace, and it is extremely important that these be refitted, otherwise oil will leak out behind the clutch. On the early type of gearbox it is essential that the ring be screwed in exactly as it was originally, otherwise the indentations will not register correctly with those on the clutch operating lever. It must be screwed in very tightly, or it will turn when operating the clutch.

The bearing for the kick-starter shaft on the clutch side is not likely to show wear, but should it be necessary to remove it it can be tapped out of position from the outside with a punch and hammer.

Checking Bearings

The selector spindle bush should be tried, together with the selector spindle. The bush is a tight fit in the housing, and is secured by four small screws.

The mainshaft is supported in the end cover by a ballrace, which can be tapped out of position quite easily. The bearing for the kick-starter shaft in the end cover is a plain cast-iron bush in the case of the two-stroke, and a bronze bearing on the o.h.c. machines. The cast-iron bush is not removable, it being cast in position in the aluminium. It should, however, not be necessary to replace it, as providing the gearbox has been well looked after, no wear will be apparent. To remove the ball bearing (on the o.h.c. machine) the bronze kick-starter shaft bush must be removed by unscrewing in a clockwise direction, as this has a left-hand thread. On late models an internal spring-loaded selector is fitted, the bush, spring and plunger being placed in the end cover.

The Selector Fork

The selector fork should now be examined. This is riveted to the inside selector lever with a special shouldered rivet. The fork should be free to revolve on the rivet, but should have no sideplay. If excessive play is present, the rivet should be replaced.

Examine all Bushes

It will be seen that the sleeve gear is fitted with a bronze bush, and this should be a good fit on the mainshaft. See that the two oil holes which pass from between the teeth to the centre bearing are clear. The teeth and the dogs of all the gears will be in perfect condition providing the gearbox has not been misused.

On very late models a special bronze bush, having oil-absorbing qualities, is fitted to the centre bearing of the low gear. On earlier models the bearing is steel to steel, with two oil grooves in the bore of the low gear. Two oilways leading from between the teeth to the oil grooves are drilled in this type, and these must not be obstructed. The pumping action of the teeth when in motion forces oil through the oil-ways to lubricate the centre bearing.

The layshaft on two-stroke models is fitted with two cast-iron bushes, by which it is supported on the kick-starter shaft. These bushes are a press fit, and should they show signs of considerable wear they should be replaced. On the o.h.c. machine a ballrace supports the layshaft on the kick-starter shaft at the large end, and the ballrace in the end cover carries the small end.

How to examine Kick-starter Parts

If the machine has been ill treated or involved in a fall on the kick-starter side of the machine, the kick-starter shaft should be examined for truth before refitting to the layshaft. The kick-starter is actuated by two rollers, which bear against a part of the kick-starter shaft and engage with serrations inside the layshaft. The rollers are supported by small springs fitted with a peg to make contact with the roller. If the springs are collapsed they should be replaced. The rollers should engage tightly with the serrations in the layshaft, but the latter should be quite free to revolve when the cam is in operation. Should the kick-starter tend to slip, larger rollers should be fitted. Oversize rollers of various sizes can be obtained from the makers for this purpose. Always use the largest size rollers possible, but be quite sure that they will allow the kick-starter to free when the releasing cam is in operation. The kick-starter cam should now be fitted to the kick-starter shaft so that the projection on the cam is on the opposite side of the shaft to the slot for the crank cotter pin.

Fig. 2.—How to change the Gear Ratios.

It is only necessary to change the layshaft and low-gear wheel. This shows the withdrawal of the low-gear wheel from the mainshaft, and the layshaft complete with kick-starter mechanism from the gearbox.

Examine the Clutch Inserts

The clutch and its operating mechanism should now receive attention. The cork inserts of the two-stroke model should project $\frac{1}{16}$ inch from the chain wheel on either side. The fabric inserts of the o.h.c. machine should project $\frac{1}{32}$ inch on either side of the plates. It should be remembered that, providing the clutch is adjusted as wear of the inserts occurs, the inserts can be used until they are nearly level with the plates on both types of machines.

And Thrust Bearing

The thrust race and thrust cup should be in good condition, but if the machine has been used with the clutch incorrectly adjusted, considerable wear will be noticeable on the parts, and the distance tube will have ridges worn upon its outer surface. In this case it is advisable to replace the parts. The seating for the spherical washer in the thrust cup should be free from ridges. The clutch springs should be straight, and if bent should be replaced.

Reassembling Gears

The method of reassembly is as follows : replace the oil-thrower washer on to the sleeve gear with the dished side facing the teeth of the gear. The gear is then pushed into position in the ballrace. The selector with fork and spindle is now placed in position, and the outside lever fitted to the square end of the spindle and secured. The middle gear should now be placed in the selector fork, with the groove for the latter nearest the gearbox end cover. The mainshaft can now be pushed through the sleeve gear and middle gear. The layshaft, complete with kick-starter mechanism, is now placed in position with the tongue of the cam bearing against the stop in the gearbox, which is to be found just below the kick-starter shaft bush on the clutch side of the machine. The low gear is now fitted to the end of the mainshaft.

Refitting End Cover—but Remember

The end-cover washer and end cover can now be fitted and secured with the end-cover bolts. In the case of gearboxes fitted with internal selector, do not forget to replace the spring and plunger. The lock nut on the end of the mainshaft should be tightened securely with a box spanner, after which the brass cap should be replaced.

Fitting Kick-starter Spring

The kick-starter crank with spring and cover should now be fitted, taking care to slide the loop at the end of the clock-type spring over the peg on the end cover. With this type of spring it is now necessary to rotate the kick-starter crank two complete turns in an anticlockwise direction to give the necessary tension to the spring. The crank cotter should then be inserted and secured with the lock nut.

Adjusting the Selector

Should the selector plunger bush have been removed from a late type of gearbox it will be necessary to readjust it. It will be noticed upon examination that the plunger hole in the bush is eccentric, and that the bush is secured in the end cover by a small setpin. Having assembled the gearbox, the outside selector lever should be pushed into top or bottom gear position. The spring-loaded plunger can be felt to engage with the notches of the selector. The plunger bush should now be rotated with a screwdriver placed in the slot for this purpose, until the lever can be pushed about $\frac{1}{16}$ inch beyond the notch. When released the lever will spring back slightly as the plunger drops to the bottom of the notch in the selector. The setpin should now be screwed in to secure the plunger bush in the end cover.

Fig. 3.—ADJUSTING THE CLUTCH.

This important operation prevents rapid wear of the clutch-operating mechanism. In the illustration the chain guard and final-drive sprocket have been removed. To adjust clutch correctly, take up the free play with the cable adjuster, screwing this out until the lever just touches the handlebar. Then turn the spring holder with the "C" spanner anticlockwise, as shown, until the clutch frees correctly when the handlebar lever is pulled up to the handlebar (see also Fig. 4).

Refitting the Clutch

The gearbox is now ready for the fitting of the clutch. In the case of late model gear-boxes, do not forget to insert the single long thrust pin in its hole in the housing before fitting the thrust cup. The thrust cup having been secured by means of the hinge clip, the thrust race can be fitted in the following order: first the distance tube is placed on the sleeve gear, and then the spherical washer against the spherical seating in the thrust cup; then the caged ballrace, and lastly the flat thrust washer.

On early type gearboxes the clutch operating lever is first engaged with the indentations of the cam ring, and the thrust cup with race then fitted in the order given above. The clutch itself must now be assembled, when it can be placed on the sleeve gear in one unit.

The Two-stroke Type

In the case of the early type of two-stroke clutch, the back plate should be laid flat on the bench and the ball bearings placed in position with the aid of grease. The chain wheel and front plate can then be placed in position. On later two-stroke machines a complete ballrace is pressed into the chain wheel, which considerably simplifies assembly.

The O.H.C. Type

With the multi-plate clutch of the o.h.c. machine, the order of re-assembly is as follows : the back plate is placed flat on the bench, next a steel plate with inserts, then a dished plate with the projections of the dished part engaging with the indentations in the back plate. The chain wheel is now placed on the centre bearing of the back plate, so that the notches in its rim drop over the projections on the plate with inserts next to the back plate.

The other dished plate is now placed in position with the dished part projecting upwards. The other steel plate with inserts is then engaged with the notches in the chain wheel, and finally the front plate. This may be rather difficult to place in position, as the projections on the dished plate below must engage with the notches in the front plate and also the projections of the back plate engaged in the slots of the front plate.

The spring holder with springs should now be screwed into the front plate. The three small thrust pins should be inserted in their holes in the back plate and held in position with the aid of grease.

Fig. 4.—Adjusting the Clutch.

This can be done as in Fig. 3 with the final-drive sprocket in position. It is not necessary to remove the chain cover.

The clutch complete can now be pushed on to the splines of the sleeve gear, the latter being supported by placing the selector lever in top gear position. The two thin steel washers should be smeared with oil and placed on the sleeve gear lock nut, when the latter can be screwed up *tightly* on to the threads of the sleeve gear. The two thin washers are of great importance, as they take the slip as the nut is rotated and prevent the springs from bending over.

The small gearbox sprocket is now fitted, taking care that it is engaged fully on the dogs of the mainshaft. The washer and lock nut should now be replaced and the latter screwed up tightly.

AUTOBOOKS WORKSHOP MANUALS

ALFA ROMEO GIULIA 1300, 1600, 1750, 2000 1962-1978 WSM
BMW 1600 1966-1973 WSM
BMW 2500, 2800, 3.0 & 3.3 1968-1977 WSM
BMW 316, 320, 320i 1975-1977 WSM
BMW 518, 520, 520i 1973-1981 WSM
FIAT 1100, 1100D, 1100R & 1200 1957-1969 WSM
FIAT 124 1966-1974 WSM
FIAT 124 SPORT 1966-1975 WSM
FIAT 125 & 125 SPECIAL 1967-1973 WSM
FIAT 126, 126L, 126 DV, 126/650 & 126/650 DV 1972-1982 WSM
FIAT 127 SALOON, SPECIAL & SPORT, 900, 1050 1971-1981 WSM
FIAT 128 1969-1982 WSM
FIAT 1300, 1500 1961-1967 WSM
FIAT 131 MIRAFIORI 1975-1982 WSM
FIAT 132 1972-1982 WSM
FIAT 500 1957-1973 WSM
FIAT 600, 600D & MULTIPLA 1955-1969 WSM
FIAT 850 1964-1972 WSM
JAGUAR MK 1, 2 1955-1969 WSM
JAGUAR S TYPE, 420 1963-1968 WSM
JAGUAR XK 120, 140, 150 MK 7, 8, 9 1948-1961 WSM
LAND ROVER 1, 2 1948-1961 WSM
MERCEDES-BENZ 190 1959-1968 WSM
MERCEDES-BENZ 220/8 1968-1972 WSM
MERCEDES-BENZ 220B 1959-1965 WSM
MERCEDES-BENZ 230 1963-1968 WSM
MERCEDES-BENZ 250 1968-1972 WSM
MERCEDES-BENZ 280 1968-1972 WSM
MINI 1959-1980 WSM
MORRIS MINOR 1952-1971 WSM
PEUGEOT 404 1960-1975 WSM
PORSCHE 911 1964-1973 WSM
PORSCHE 911 1970-1977 WSM
RENAULT 16 1965-1979 WSM
RENAULT 8, 10, 1100 1962-1971 WSM
ROVER 3500, 3500S 1968-1976 WSM
SUNBEAM RAPIER, ALPINE 1955-1965 WSM
TRIUMPH SPITFIRE, GT6, VITESSE 1962-1968 WSM
TRIUMPH TR4, TR4A 1961-1967 WSM
VOLKSWAGEN BEETLE 1968-1977 WSM

VELOCEPRESS AUTOMOBILE BOOKS & MANUALS

ABARTH BUYERS GUIDE
AUSTIN-HEALEY 6-CYLINDER WSM
AUSTIN-HEALEY SPRITE & MG MIDGET 1958-1971 WSM
BMW 600 LIMOUSINE FACTORY WSM
BMW 600 LIMOUSINE OWNERS HAND BOOK & SERVICE MANUAL
BMW 2000 & 2002 1966-1976 WSM
BMW ISETTA FACTORY WSM
BOOK OF THE CARRERA PANAMERICANA - MEXICAN ROAD RACE
COMPLETE CATALOG OF JAPANESE MOTOR VEHICLES
CORVAIR 1960-1969 OWNERS WORKSHOP MANUAL
CORVETTE V8 1955-1962 OWNERS WORKSHOP MANUAL
DIALED IN - THE JAN OPPERMAN STORY
FERRARI 250/GT SERVICE AND MAINTENANCE
FERRARI 308 SERIES BUYER'S AND OWNER'S GUIDE
FERRARI BERLINETTA LUSSO
FERRARI BROCHURES AND SALES LITERATURE 1946-1967
FERRARI BROCHURES AND SALES LITERATURE 1968-1989
FERRARI GUIDE TO PERFORMANCE
FERRARI OPP, MAINTENANCE & SERVICE H/BOOKS 1948-1963
FERRARI OWNER'S HANDBOOK
FERRARI SERIAL NUMBERS PART I - ODD NUMBERS TO 21399
FERRARI SERIAL NUMBERS PART II - EVEN NUMBERS TO 1050
FERRARI SPYDER CALIFORNIA
FERRARI TUNING TIPS & MAINTENANCE TECHNIQUES
HENRY'S FABULOUS MODEL "A" FORD
HOW TO BUILD A FIBERGLASS CAR
HOW TO BUILD A RACING CAR
HOW TO RESTORE THE MODEL 'A' FORD
IF HEMINGWAY HAD WRITTEN A RACING NOVEL
JAGUAR E-TYPE 3.8 & 4.2 WSM
LE MANS 24 (THE BOOK THAT THE FILM WAS BASED ON)
MASERATI BROCHURES AND SALES LITERATURE
MASERATI OWNER'S HANDBOOK
METROPOLITAN FACTORY WSM
MGA & MGB OWNERS HANDBOOK & WSM
MG MIDGET TC, TD, TF & TF1500 WORKSHOP MANUAL
OBERT'S FIAT GUIDE
PERFORMANCE TUNING THE SUNBEAM TIGER
PORSCHE 356 1948-1965 WSM
PORSCHE 912 WSM
SOUPING THE VOLKSWAGEN
SOLEX CARBURETORS (EMPHASIS ON UK & EU AUTOMOBILES)
SU CARBURETORS (EMPHASIS ON UK AUTOMOBILES)
TRIUMPH TR2, TR3, TR4 1953-1965 WSM
TUNING FOR SPEED (P.E. IRVING)
VEDA ORR'S NEW REVISED HOT ROD PICTORIAL
VOLKSWAGEN TRANSPORTER, TRUCKS, STATION WAGONS WSM
VOLVO 1944-1968 ALL MODELS WSM
WEBER CARBURETORS (EMPHASIS ON ALFA & FIAT)

BROOKLANDS BOOKS & ROAD TEST PORTFOLIOS (RTP)

AC CARS 1904-2009
ALFA ROMEO 1920-1933 ROAD TEST PORTFOLIO
ALFA ROMEO 1934-1940 ROAD TEST PORTFOLIO
BRABHAM RALT HONDA THE RON TAURANAC STORY
BUGATTI TYPE 10 TO TYPE 40 ROAD TEST PORTFOLIO
BUGATTI TYPE 10 TO TYPE 251 ROAD TEST PORTFOLIO
BUGATTI TYPE 41 TO TYPE 55 ROAD TEST PORTFOLIO
BUGATTI TYPE 57 TO TYPE 251 ROAD TEST PORTFOLIO
DELAHAYE ROAD TEST PORTFOLIO
FERRARI ROAD CARS 1946-1956 ROAD TEST PORTFOLIO
FIAT 500 1936-1972 ROAD TEST PORTFOLIO
FIAT DINO ROAD TEST PORTFOLIO
HISPANO SUIZA ROAD TEST PORTFOLIO
HONDA ST1100/ST1300 PAN EUROPEAN 1990-2002 RTP
JAGUAR MK1 & MK2 ROAD TEST PORTFOLIO
LOTUS CORTINA ROAD TEST PORTFOLIO
MV AGUSTA F4 750 & 1000 1997-2007 ROAD TEST PORTFOLIO
TATRA CARS ROAD TEST PORTFOLIO

VELOCEPRESS MOTORCYCLE BOOKS & MANUALS

1930'S BRITISH MOTORCYCLE GEARBOXES & CLUTCHES (BOOK OF)
AJS SINGLES & TWINS 250cc THRU 1000cc 1932-1948 (BOOK OF)
AJS SINGLES 1955-65 350cc & 500cc (BOOK OF)
AJS SINGLES 1945-60 350cc & 500cc MODELS 16 & 18 (BOOK OF)
ARIEL 1939-1960 4 STROKE SINGLES (BOOK OF)
ARIEL LEADER & ARROW 1958-1964 (BOOK OF)
ARIEL MOTORCYCLES 1933-1951 WSM
ARIEL PREWAR MODELS 1932-1939 (BOOK OF)
BMW M/CYCLES R26 R27 (1956-1967) FACTORY WSM
BMW M/CYCLES R50 R50S R60 R69S (1955-1969) FACTORY WSM
BSA BANTAM ALL MODELS FROM 1948 ONWARDS (BOOK OF)
BSA SINGLES & V-TWINS UP TO 1927 (BOOK OF)
BSA SINGLES & V-TWINS 1936-1939 (BOOK OF)
BSA SINGLES & V-TWINS 1936-1952 (BOOK OF)
BSA OHV & SV SINGLES 250-600cc 1945-1954 (BOOK OF)
BSA OHV & SV SINGLES - 250cc 1954-1970 (BOOK OF)
BSA OHV SINGLES 350 & 500cc 1955-1967 (BOOK OF)
BSA TWINS 1948-1962 (BOOK OF)
BSA TWINS 1962-1969 (SECOND BOOK OF)
CATALOG OF BRITISH MOTORCYCLES (1951 MODELS)
DOUGLAS PRE-WAR ALL MODELS 1929-1939 (BOOK OF)
DOUGLAS POST-WAR ALL MODELS 1948-1957 FACTORY WSM
DUCATI 160cc, 250cc & 350cc OHC MODELS FACTORY WSM
HONDA 50 ALL MODELS UP TO 1970 INC MONKEY & TRAIL (BOOK OF)
HONDA 90 ALL MODELS UP TO 1966 (BOOK OF)
HONDA MOTORCYCLES 125-150 TWINS C/CS/CB/CA WSM
HONDA MOTORCYCLES 250-305 TWINS C/CS/CB WSM
HONDA MOTORCYCLES C100 SUPER CUB WSM
HONDA MOTORCYCLES C110 SPORT CUB 1962-1969 WSM
HONDA TWINS & SINGLES 50cc THRU 305cc 1960-1966 (BOOK OF)
HONDA TWINS ALL MODELS 125cc THRU 450cc UP TO 1968 (BOOK OF)
INDIAN PONYBIKE, BOY RACER & PAPOOSE ILL PARTS LIST & SALES LIT
J.A.P. ENGINES 1927-1952 & MOTORCYCLES 1934-1952 (BOOK OF)
LAMBRETTA ALL 125 & 150cc MODELS 1947-1957 (BOOK OF)
LAMBRETTA LI & TV MODELS 1957-1970 (SECOND BOOK OF)
MATCHLESS 350 & 500cc SINGLES 1945-1956 (BOOK OF)
MATCHLESS 350 & 500cc SINGLES 1955-1966 (BOOK OF)
MOTORCYCLE ENGINEERING (P. E. Irving)
NORTON 1932-1947 (BOOK OF)
NORTON 1938-1956 (BOOK OF)
NORTON DOMINATOR TWINS 1955-1965 (BOOK OF)
NORTON MODELS 19, 50 & ES2 1955-1965 (BOOK OF)
NORTON MOTORCYCLES 1957-1970 FACTORY WSM
NORTON PREWAR MODELS 1932-1939 (BOOK OF)
NSU PRIMA ALL MODELS 1956-1964 (BOOK OF)
NSU QUICKLY ALL MODELS 1953-1963 (BOOK OF)
RALEIGH MOPEDS 1960-1969 (BOOK OF)
RALEIGH MOTORCYCLES 1919-1933 (BOOK OF)
ROYAL ENFIELD SINGLES & V TWINS 1934-1946 (BOOK OF)
ROYAL ENFIELD SINGLES & V TWINS 1937-1953 (BOOK OF)
ROYAL ENFIELD SINGLES 1946-1962 (BOOK OF)
ROYAL ENFIELD 736cc INTERCEPTOR FACTORY WSM
ROYAL ENFIELD 250cc & 350cc SINGLES 1958-1966 (SECOND BOOK OF)
RUDGE MOTORCYCLES 1933-1939 (BOOK OF)
SPEED AND HOW TO OBTAIN IT
SUNBEAM MOTORCYCLES 1928-1939 (BOOK OF)
SUNBEAM S7 & S8 1946-1957 (BOOK OF)
SUZUKI 50cc & 80cc UP TO 1966 (BOOK OF)
SUZUKI T10 1963-1967 FACTORY WSM
SUZUKI T20 & T200 1965-1969 FACTORY WSM
TRIUMPH PRE-WAR MOTORCYCLE 1935-1939 (BOOK OF)
TRIUMPH MOTORCYCLES 1935-1949 (BOOK OF)
TRIUMPH MOTORCYCLES 1937-1951 WSM
TRIUMPH MOTORCYCLES 1945-1955 FACTORY WSM
TRIUMPH TWINS 1945-1958 (BOOK OF)
TRIUMPH TWINS 1956-1969 (BOOK OF)
VELOCETTE ALL SINGLES & TWINS 1925-1970 (BOOK OF)
VESPA 1951-1961 (BOOK OF)
VESPA 125 & 150cc & GS MODELS 1955-1963 (SECOND BOOK OF)
VESPA 90, 125 & 150cc 1963-1972 (THIRD BOOK OF)
VESPA GS & SS 1955-1968 (BOOK OF)
VILLIERS ENGINE (BOOK OF)
VINCENT MOTORCYCLES 1935-1955 WSM

FOR A DETAILED DESCRIPTION OF ANY OF OUR TITLES PLEASE VISIT OUR WEBSITE
www.VelocePress.com

NOTES

Lightning Source UK Ltd.
Milton Keynes UK
UKHW020843160720
366630UK00006B/247